INVISIBLE TEACHING

D1343824

INVISIBLE TEACHING

101 *ish* ways to create energy, openness and focus in the classroom

Dave Keeling and David Hodgson

Crown House Publishing Limited
www.crownhouse.co.uk - www.crownhousepublishing.com

First published by

Crown House Publishing Ltd
Crown Buildings, Bancyfelin, Carmarthen,
Wales, SA33 5ND, UK
www.crownhouse.co.uk

and

Crown House Publishing Company LLC
6 Trowbridge Drive, Suite 5, Bethel, CT 06801, USA
www.crownhousepublishing.com

British Library Cataloguing-in-Publication Data
A catalogue entry for this book is available
from the British Library.

Print ISBN 978-184590685-6
Mobi ISBN 978-184590743-3
ePub ISBN 978-184590744-0
LCCN 2010937329

Printed and bound in the UK by
Bell & Bain Ltd, Glasgow

Acknowledgements

David and Dave would like to thank all at Crown House Publishing for their continuing and unwavering support in all aspects of bringing this work to an audience. They would also like to thank Trevor Keeling, Jim Hamilton, Claire Fowler, Chris Delaney, Ryan Philpott, Cathy Hodgson and Steph Davies for their help, ideas, friendship and laughs.

A special mention must go to Big Dave Harris, head teacher of NUSA (Nottingham University Samworth Academy) for allowing us the freedom to experiment with our ideas by using his inspiring school, great students and tremendous on-site catering!

Contents

Intro

We recently explained to a colleague the ideas behind *Invisible Teaching*.

'I can see it on the shelves already,' he announced enthusiastically.

'Oops' we replied. 'That sort of defeats the object.'

Or does it?

What we are trying to say is this. Not everyone who saunters past this book will be able to see it. It will appear invisible to them based on how they view themselves, their job and the world they inhabit.

If you want to work more and play less, you will *not* see it.

If you love your subject and yet hate kids, you will *not* see it.

If you only have eyes for Dan Brown's latest, histrionic, Masonic, monastic mystery then you will *not* see it.

But if your desire is to challenge yourself, to put your students first, to prepare them for the world in which they will live and work by blazing a trail as a first rate example of what a twenty-first century learner should look like, then not only will you see it but you will pick up this book, return home and immediately begin reading it.

Congratulations, you have passed the first test. Welcome to *Invisible Teaching*. You're in. Game on!

This book is not about doing things harder or necessarily better, but it is definitely about doing something different. In order to shift from a place of comfort, so that we can continue to evolve and grow, there is a need for all of us to challenge ourselves to do something different.

Our children are comfortable, they have been spoon-fed their entire educational lives, but instead of being well-nourished and hungry for more there is a tendency for most students to leave apathetically fat; stuffed full of information that will do them little good when they leave the education system and with the firm belief that if they sit still for long enough, somehow someone or something will sort them out.

We believe that this book encourages both students and teachers alike to engage with and develop three key areas: *energy, openness* and *focus*. The formula for engagement, according to leading paediatric neurologist Dr Andrew Curran is as follows. We need to feel understood; if we feel understood, our self-esteem soars. If our self-esteem soars, our confidence grows. If our confidence grows we will engage. Conversely, if we do not feel understood our self-esteem plummets, our confidence goes, we disengage and we are potentially lost forever.

We want to take you through a process of engagement, to blend the qualities of energy, openness and focus and bring this all together and discover that special moment – the moment of *flow*. You know when it has happened. You feel it and you may even catch a glimpse of it; a moment, a brief flicker of light, a spark of joy, a ray of hope in the eyes of your students.

This is the moment when something magical happens – the transformation of invisible to visible.

This is the moment when you are no longer simply working for a living but discovering the capacity to guide, support, enthuse, inform, inspire and impact the minds of your students. You are no longer just a teacher – you have become so much more.

The word *enthusiasm* literally means 'the god within' and, without any reference to religion, it still invokes the feeling of spirit, and that is what we want to see when we are working with others. We want to spot the light behind the eyes, the signs that they are actively engaged in their own life and love of learning rather than passively waiting for something more interesting to come along.

Allowing the principles of invisible teaching to permeate throughout your work will encourage your students to become the learners they need to be in a world that is rapidly changing. Qualifications may be the down payment or deposit for a good life, but the real currency of this century is flexibility, adaptability and versatility.

In a world full of change the learners will inherit the earth, while the knowers will find themselves beautifully equipped to deal with a world that no longer exists.

Eric Hoffer

Change is not merely necessary for life, it is life.

Alvin Toffler

One thing you will need for this book to work for you is courage. To be a true twenty-first century teacher you will be required to be more courageous than your students and your colleagues because invisible teaching can only truly be effective if we summon up the bravery to do something new. It will at times feel uncertain, scary and uncomfortable. But growing up always has been.

As Derren Brown said recently, 'Courage is not the absence of fear but the mastery of it.'

What is Invisible Teaching?

What is Invisible Teaching?

First, we need to understand that we can't always see everything that is real, such as:

Oxygen
Stars during the day
Love
Potential
Dark matter – it holds the entire universe together and we don't know what it is!
The future/time
What others think
The point (sometimes)
The wood for the trees (joke)
Light – we can only see what it reflects off
Electricity

We visit around 200 schools per year. We see brilliant teachers in their classrooms and are fascinated by the magic they create. We, like other teachers, wonder what it is these brilliant teachers do. In great magic and in great teaching the important stuff is hidden – invisible.

Invisible qualities the best teachers bring to the classroom

This list has been collated from children's responses when asked what makes a good teacher:

Confidence
Respect
Always in control
Making lessons interesting
Fairness

Present (involving students and reacting to questions not just sticking to a script)

Funny

Knowledgeable (without making you feel stupid)

Kind and sometimes tough

Original (surprising us with new ways of doing things)

Teachers with these qualities will have worked out the necessity for energy, openness and focus and how to pass these on to their students. The list reminds us that: *how you teach is more important than what you teach.*

Your job is no longer to teach. Your job is that they learn.

Ian Gilbert

Brilliant teachers have high brand value

Value is mostly perception. Most of the value of a product is perception rather than actual worth; the power of brand. Coca-Cola probably doesn't taste very different to other cola drinks. Similarly, brilliant teachers have a high brand value. They may look like other teachers but they are different. Their brand is developed through their authenticity, their charisma, their positive values and their day-to-day behaviour in school.

Products are advertised relentlessly to develop brand identity and awareness. Teachers build their brand identity every day by the way they walk in and out of school, smile and talk to students (or not) in the corridor, give feedback or ask questions. All of these tiny things are like thirty-second TV adverts which help to create the brand. Popular and good teachers do all of these small things which are invisible in terms of the timetable and lesson content.

Do you know how the students or other teachers view you and your teaching? What would they say about you? What sort of brand would you be?

Cillit Bang, a no-nonsense teacher who gets the job done without fuss and fanfare: bang, grade C and the child is gone.

Compare the Meerkat, the attractive, popular, young new teacher that all the kids are talking about. Will they remain popular when the novelty wears off?

DFS, the comfortable old teacher who wants an easy, quiet life and always has a sale offer: be quiet and you'll get 50% off your homework, offer ends soon.

We Buy Any Car Dot Com/Go Compare, the annoying, loud, shouty teacher who repeats a couple of well-tried mantras ad nauseam: 'If you don't work hard you'll end up in a dead end job', 'I'm quite happy to give out a whole class detention', 'You're wasting your own time'.

Werther's Original, the teacher nearing retirement who is counting down the days and reminisces to students about the good old halcyon days of teaching when corporal punishment filled the corridors with fear, only to be interrupted by occasional yelps of pain.

L'Oréal, the teacher who does everything for their students; because they're worth it. In fact, they do so much for their students that the students leave unable to do anything for themselves.

No Win, No Fee, the teacher without responsibility for events in their classroom who blames anyone but themself: the government, the school building, the students, rap music, the parents.

How are you developing your brand? What would your tagline be?

If Carlsberg made teachers, they'd probably make teachers like me.

Teach it, learn it, Argos it.

You can't get better than a Slick-Fit teacher.

Brilliant teachers make their students feel good about themselves

Students are generally very accommodating. If they are told they are stupid they will behave accordingly. They know if they are in the bottom maths group or top English set and this has a massive impact.

Low caste individuals have corrosive expectations that they import into the experiment when their caste is made salient.

Karla Hoff World Bank, 2004 (Wilkinson & Pickett, 2010)

A couple of researchers tested 600 12-year-old boys in India (Wilkinson & Pickett, 2010). The scores were collected. The boys were then asked to introduce themselves, revealing their caste and social status to the whole group. Afterwards, all of the boys were retested. The scores of the high caste boys went up from an average of 55 to 61 (a 10% increase). The scores of the low caste boys dropped from 56 to 42 (a 25% fall).

This is a powerful invisible force in the classroom. Brilliant teachers find ways to make their students feel good about themselves. They generally incorporate variety in their lessons. Variety of delivery method, styles and ways to learn (such as multiple intelligences and VAK (visual, auditory and kinaesthetic)) plus a mixture of assessment methods all give more students a chance to shine. Unfortunately, there is pressure for teachers to narrow the curriculum and the teaching methods they use. The best teachers resist this pressure.

Brilliant teachers understand the importance of energy, openness and focus

These are the three elements of invisible teaching that can really boost your classroom performance.

Energy

The dictionary definition of energy is 'intensity or vitality of action or expression'.

Energy is contagious.

Are you a radiator or a drain?

Who or what gives you energy?

Energy cannot be created or destroyed, it can only change from one form to another.

People don't like to destroy what they have helped to create.

Calm energy is good for us. Controlling the flow of energy as waves of relaxation down our bodies and focusing our attention on the inside can improve our mood and performance.

Can you go from knowing it to doing it?

We can all come up with ten reasons not to do something but can you come up with twelve reasons to do it?

The ebb and flow of energy levels in a classroom can seem random and beyond control. Not so for invisible teachers; they seamlessly blend the level of energy in the room with the lesson content as closely as a dancer and her shadow.

High energy	Low energy
Action	Calm
Networking	Remembering
Excitement	Absorbing
Fun	Modelling
Vitality	Relaxing

The fireworks

High energy activities generate movement, action, laughter, fun, excitement and interest. They are used to start a session, a new topic or an idea. Great teachers control and direct the energy created by issuing instructions and learning points as the activity progresses.

Undirected energisers are the equivalent of bringing the wildness and chaos of the playground into the classroom. This sort of energy is difficult to control and some teachers fear bringing this type of energy into their classrooms to avoid this happening; the result is dull and monotonous lessons. When high energy activities are used well they develop openness or focus – they are powerful and effective.

If you want to raise the energy in your classroom look for the activities with this icon

These are perfect for you to increase the energy in a controlled way.

Drift into an altered state

Low energy activities are the equivalent of a group of warriors sitting around a campfire listening to stories from the shaman as they drift into an altered state. Brain scans show that the pattern of alpha waves generated when we are in a relaxed state, as opposed to normal waking state beta waves, enhances learning, retention and recall. Setting up a campfire in your classroom may break just too many health and safety rules, so the modern equivalent is a clip from YouTube, a

DVD, a piece of music or a teacher-led discussion. In these moments teachers invite students to go inside to think.

When questions have no wrong answers they are more powerful. *The invisible teacher encourages students to share what they think rather than what they know.*

Low energy activities linked to developing openness or focus are the most powerful. When we relax we switch on our internal dialogue and recall, recite and formulate new concepts and wonder.

Mirror neurons have demonstrated the importance of learning by observation. When watching a game of tennis mirror neurons inside our brains fire in sequences and make connections as if we were actually playing. We become better tennis players just from watching Andy Murray play (except in Grand Slam finals when he's not very good).

To lower energy in your classroom look for activities with this icon

Openness at one end and focus on the other

Henry Ford famously said that if he'd listened to his customers he'd have developed a faster horse. Instead he used his imagination to invent the motor car and changed the course of human history. He was open to new ways of thinking. He followed this with incredible application and focus to ensure his invention was practical and marketable. Successful entrepreneurs usually demonstrate the ability to combine openness and focus to create new and profitable businesses. On programmes like *Dragons' Den* we often see people pitching ideas that have either openness or focus but not both. They are usually greeted with 'I'm out'. Invisible teachers develop both in their students.

Focus	Openness
Plan	Creative
Purpose/conviction	Imagination
Detail	Possibilities
Steps	Flexible
Understanding and applying rules	Bending existing or making new rules

Positive openness

Positive openness is the joy of experiencing new things for the first time or familiar things with fresh eyes.

Openness can also be expressed negatively. The clichéd hippy drifting through life from India to Glastonbury to Peru and back to Glastonbury (I have the photos) could be eternally open to possibility, potential, growth and experience yet have nothing to show for it other than a dog on a rope and a tie-dyed hemp pullover. Dreaming is great but without focus it is unfulfilled potential flushed down the toilet.

Openness

In order to be creative you must first be open.

When was the last time you embraced something totally new?

If life is like an open book which page are you on right now?

If you are open people will visit.

Are you a grown-up or are
you still growing up?

We do not stop playing because we grow old;
we grow old because we stop playing.

You can't polish a turd but
you can roll it in glitter.

Which do you say most: 'Yes but' or 'Yes and'?

If you are the problem,
you are the solution.

Take a breath, smile and imagine you could
learn something new.

For activities that develop positive openness in your class-room look out for this icon

Positive focus

Positive focus is all about planning, but planning in specific ways.

When we think we are in danger (perceived or real) our stress response engulfs our mind and body. Cortisol and adrenaline flood our system and puts us in an alert state, ready for fight, flight, flock or freeze. The result is good in the short term – allowing us to deal with the danger – but terrible in the long term as it can often be deployed as a defence mechanism, shutting us off from new experiences and opportunities. Many nasty diseases are linked to the over-use of the stress response. This is an example of focus at its worst. We are focused on the one thing in front of us and oblivious to everything else. It is like driving a car in first gear all the time – lots of power at a high cost of fuel and damage to the engine. (Thanks to my wife for this analogy during the long months she learned to drive in my car.) We can take a positive from every situation.

Focus

You have twenty-four hours – what are you going to do to fill it?

If you don't know what you want, how are you going to get it?

Why do you do what you do?

When was the last time you were so focused you forgot what you were doing?

How good are you at unlearning something and then relearning it because the knowledge has changed?

Do you focus mostly on what you want or what you don't want?

The first rule of focus is 'wherever you are be there'.

How often are you out of focus?

Is it better to do one thing really well or fifty things alright?

Do you focus on the process or the outcome?

For activities that develop positive focus in your classroom look out for this icon

The dance between openness and focus is required for learning a new skill

How do people really learn? It is in essence a movement along a continuum that is openness at one end and focus at the other. It is our ability to make sense of ideas at one end and facts at the other. Invisible teachers show students the value of both and the opportunity to develop both.

Babies and young children tend to do openness and focus really well. We learn so much in the first five years of life that we don't have time to be closed to new experiences.

We like the following definition from Guy Claxton in *What's the Point of School?* It sums up the dance between openness and focus required for learning a new skill.

1   They watch how other people do things and consider adapting it to their own style.

2   They go off by themselves and practise the hard parts.

3   They ask their own questions at their own pace and select their own teacher.

4   They imagine and try out possible solutions that are not finished, polished theories.

5   They reject some ideas and adapt others.

6   They imagine how they can apply the skill in future situations.

We all need imagination and plans, skill and the flexibility to apply this. Otherwise we enter a false debate about which one is more important. On the *Today* programme on Radio 4, Michael Gove recently argued that students need to learn more facts. His reasoning: when he was a researcher on *Today* his job was to research a story and provide facts to the journalist who could then use these to prepare good questions for an interview. This is OK, but surely we are also responsible for teaching children to assess the quality of their research so they don't rely on dodgy facts. Using one entry on Wikipedia may not be reliable. How we use facts to create our view of the world is important. The process of turning information into meaning is the interplay of openness and focus. If this is close to the definition of learning; it is also close to the definition of being human.

We would like to share over 100 of our favourite activities with you that include the essential ingredients of energy, openness and focus – and demonstrate invisible teaching at its best. Our advice is to take a breath, smile and imagine you could learn something new.

Be fearless, not fearful

Be visibly invisible

Be yourself

Be-gin.

Activities for Students

1 Mexican Stand-Off

Time: 5 mins

Additional Resources: none

Students attempt to beat the teacher in an energetic quick-draw competition

A fast and quick energiser that gets the whole group buzzing and focused for the beginning of a session.

The teacher invites the class to stand and make their hands into pretend guns which they must then place by their sides as if they were holstered. The teacher will then ask them to draw their guns accompanied with a very vocal 'bang'.

The object of the game is for the class to draw quicker than the teacher.

Great fun can be had by building the tension between each stand-off. For extra pleasure you may wish to experiment with a varying array of handlebar moustaches and Mexican costumes.

2 Paper Tails

Time: 5 mins

Additional Resources: one newspaper

Students learn strategy in a speedy game of cat and mouse

Clear a space and tear the newspaper into as many strips as there are students. Each student must then tuck the strip of paper into the top of their trousers/skirt, as if they have a tail.

The object of the game is to try and remove as many of your classmates' tails as possible whilst keeping your own tail intact. Once your tail has been removed (it hurts just writing that) you are out. The winner is the person left at the end with their tail in place.

This game requires students to employ physical dexterity, energy, risk and strategy as they must quickly decide when to attack and when to defend. It is also huge fun and a great way to use up your Sunday supplements.

You're Fired, You're Hired

Time: 10 mins

Additional Resources: none

Students justify their place within education and learn to focus on how important it is to make a positive contribution

Announce to the group that to be educated is no longer a right in this country and that the school is now a business and the students are its workforce. Then pose this question: 'The school has decided to fire all of the students. Based on your current attitudes and behaviour come up with the three reasons the school gave for your dismissal and then counter-balance this argument by coming up with three reasons why the school should re-hire you. What have you contributed to the school environment as a student and what makes you an invaluable member of your school?'

This is harder than it sounds and over the last six months we have asked this question many times to hundreds of students and can count the genuine responses on both hands. A student recently responded to the question by shouting out that the school should keep him because he was 'Brilliant'. Unfortunately for him there was no evidence within the school to back up that comment. On the other hand, a female student answered this question by explaining that she supports her fellow students when she can, gets involved with lots of extra-curricular activities and tries to contribute as much as she can.

Most students do not recognise how lucky they are to have been handed their education on a plate (and in a lot of cases a new building). This activity challenges the students' attitudes towards learning and their school and how it may be perceived by others. It also encourages them to look at the skills and abilities they do have and how they may bring these to the fore.

The point is that if they cannot justify their position in an environment that has to keep them, then how on earth will they be able to justify their position in a working world that doesn't?

The Flying Feather

Time: 10–15 mins

Additional Resources: two to six feathers (or balloons)

Students practise energy, openness and focus in this fun game as teams keep a feather (or balloon) in the air

Divide the group into teams of six to ten. Each team should stand in a circle. Students must keep the feather in the air by blowing it when it comes near them. The best ones to use are the small duck feathers found in pillows. If the feather touches the floor the person nearest to it throws it back into the air. If the feather touches someone they are out of the round. The winner is the last person to be touched by the feather.

A balloon can be used as a substitute item in this game.

The Flow Test

Time: 5–10 mins

Additional Resources: none

Students learn about flow and when they achieve it in their own lives by completing a quick quiz

Mihaly Csikszentmihalyi (pronounced *me-high cheeks-sent-me-high*) offers adults a way of assessing flow – the degree to which we are 'in the zone' during specific activities. Richard

Reeves, writer on all things related to happiness, defines flow as the moment when we're so absorbed in a task that we stick out our tongue without knowing it. Children do it whilst colouring in. If it's good enough for adults, it's good enough for teenagers too.

Think of an activity and when you were last feeling flow.

	Yes	No
Did you have a feeling of 'this is the real me'?	☐	☐
Were you excited?	☐	☐
Were you disappointed when you had finished?	☐	☐
Did you think about ways you could do more of the activity or ways you could develop your skill or experience within the activity?	☐	☐
Did you feel energised rather than exhausted?	☐	☐
Did you lose track of real time (time passed more quickly)?	☐	☐

The more yes answers you give to the above questions the higher the flow. People generally do not report high flow whilst watching TV.

This checklist is an excellent way to measure flow (a combination of energy, openness and focus) and identify which parts are low and in need of a reset. We can experience flow in a wide range of activities such as walks, sport, leisure activities, drawing, reading and enjoying good food or company.

⑥ Superhero

Time: 10 mins

Additional Resources: paper and pens

Students create an alter ego

The reason that education is one of the hardest jobs these days is that we are attempting to educate students for a world in which we have no real idea of what they will actually be doing. What we can do, though, is challenge their thinking and encourage them to explore the idea that nothing is impossible and that creativity is endless.

The students have five minutes to invent a superhero and name five superpowers that makes them super.

Here is a superhero we prepared earlier:

Name: Dangerous Dave

Superpower 1: Never gets hurt

Superpower 2: Can heal people

Superpower 3:
Can appear and disappear at will

Superpower 4: Really big muscles
(back off, I've never had any!)

Superpower 5: Ability to fly

You may like to suggest that the students accompany their list with a picture or at the very least a costume design.

This activity enables the students to be creative, open-minded and above all allows them to entertain the idea of possibility.

7 Have-a-Go Hero

Time: 10–15 mins

Additional Resources: paper and pens

Linking this to the Superhero activity above, the students are required to take a step back from their superhero and one step closer to themselves

Ask the students to imagine they are a superhero in training. They have five assessment levels to pass before they can become a fully-fledged, cape-wearing crime fighter.

They are currently level 1. In groups ask them to come up with activities that could help with their training and begin to develop the sorts of skills that will eventually manifest themselves as the chosen superpowers.

For instance, from the example provided in Activity 6:

1 'Never gets hurt' becomes wears protective clothing and thinks about and plans what they are going to do before rushing into it.

2 'Can heal people' becomes begins training with the St John Ambulance and learns basic first aid.

3 'Can appear and disappear at will' becomes turning up at the right time and fully prepared so you don't feel the need to 'do one' whenever it gets uncomfortable.

4 'Really big muscles' becomes using the gym membership you pay for rather than just looking at it, perhaps having the occasional chocolate protein shake and watching *Pumping Iron* and *Rocky III* back to back.

5 'Ability to fly' becomes Google search 'adrenaline junkie' and pursue at your leisure any of these

sporting endeavours: hang gliding, base jumping, paragliding, free running, gliding, bungee jumping, parachuting, cliff diving, wearing jet packs, wing walking, trampolining and becoming a human cannonball.

This activity goes to prove that even superheroes have to start some-where; that small steps and practice are the keys to developing skills; and that you don't just become great at something overnight – it starts today so that in the future you will be better prepared and able to fight the good fight.

Better than 'Hi' or 'Hello'

Time: 5 mins

Additional Resources: none

Students explore one of the most basic human needs – being noticed and acknowledged face to face (without the use of mobile phones)

People like to feel they are noticed, acknowledged and respected. The film *Avatar* borrows a two-part Zulu greeting: when people first meet they look each other in the eye and one says, 'I am here to be seen'. The other nods and replies with, 'I see you'. This is a great start to an interaction between people.

The only way to prove this is a superior greeting is to ask students to try it out. The modern 'Hello' or 'Hi' is not so good. According to Stephen Fry on *QI* the word hello was invented to start telephone conversations because originally there were long pauses following a line connection by an operator.

Agree an appropriate greeting for the class. In the past, teachers would be greeted by a class standing to attention as they entered a classroom and students would sit after the teacher acknowledged the gesture.

Robert Holden, in Success Intelligence, *says he uses this as an activity on his courses and asks attendees to greet around ten people using this method. It can be very powerful because being noticed and accepted for who we are is a fundamental part of being human.*

⑨ Say What You See

Time: 5–10 mins preparation time, then a further 5 mins in class

Additional Resources: a little research around the school with a mobile phone/camera or good old-fashioned pen and paper

Students learn the power of focus by trying to identify common features and landmarks around the school – more difficult and more fun than you might think

Version 1

Walk around the school looking at familiar things with fresh eyes. Make a list of things including their colour, shape and position. Ask students the following types of questions to assess their awareness of their environment:

Activities for Students

What colour is the door to the staffroom?

How many chairs are on the stage?

What shape is the reception area?

What is the doormat in the reception area made from and how big is it?

What colour are the curtains in the hall?

What shape/how many tables are there in the lunch hall?

Which is taller: the sports hall or the roof of the languages block?

Which is further from the car park: the science or the English blocks?

Which chairs are more comfortable: the dining hall or assembly hall?

What kind of tree stands nearest the school gates?

Extend the idea to other things:

Do you know the colour of your toothbrush?

What colour are your pants (without looking)?*

*What duvet cover is on your bed today?***

*Unfortunately the colour of many teenagers' pants is no mystery as they wear their trousers so low it is a relief that 'going commando' is not popular these days.

**If it's Postman Pat or the Teletubbies, and your student is in Year 10 with a hard-man reputation to maintain, you suggest they pretend to forget.

Version 2

A similar version of this activity is the teacher takes photographs, perhaps on a mobile phone, of close-ups of familiar places around the school and asks the students to identify the location. It is best if the photo can be displayed on a screen for the whole group to see. Alternatively, the teacher could ask the students to take a photo to challenge the rest of the class.

10 Three and One

Time: 3 mins

Additional Resources: none

Students turn up with a reason to be there

At the beginning of the lesson ask the students in pairs to focus on three things they would like to gain from the lesson (fun, learn something new and cash are the top three we encounter on a regular basis) and one thing they do not want (to be bored is the most frequent answer).

Armed with this information the teacher can then craft a lesson that has the buy-in from the students as it is they who have generated the objectives and direction. This is an incredibly useful technique for anyone to quickly ascertain the mood and desire of a group.

This activity gives the power back to students and asks them to take some responsibility for their learning.

11 Fight or Flight

Time: 10 mins

Additional Resources: A4 paper

Students practise energy, openness and focus in this competitive game in which individuals attempt to make the paper aeroplane that will fly furthest. In the process they learn an interesting lesson about the role risk plays in life

Ask the group to each make a paper aeroplane using a sheet of A4. Offer the group a challenge within the following rules of engagement:

- Ask each person to take their plane and stand touching the wall at the back of the class.
- Each person is only allowed one throw.
- The person whose plane touches the wall opposite without it touching the floor, ceiling or other walls/ windows from the furthest distance is the winner.

- Each person can choose how close to stand to the target wall.
- Ask people to throw in order of height or oldest to youngest.

The safe thing to do is stand close to the target wall to ensure a hit. The high risk strategy is to throw from a long distance – increasing the chance of winning if you hit the target but decreasing the chances of hitting the target at all. Usually boys risk more than girls in this activity.

Life is about balancing risk and safety. The skill is to work out the rules for each of life's challenges. People throwing later have an advantage over those throwing earlier. This replicates the value of experience in life. Energy, openness and focus are required for success in this activity.

12 Wrong Hand, Right Hand

Time: 10 mins

Additional Resources: none

Students practise energy, openness and focus in this energetic game in which they learn that habits can be liberating or constraining whilst putting on their socks and shoes with their wrong hands

Ask students to remove their socks and shoes. Working alone they must put on their socks and shoes but they can only use one hand (their non-preferred hand, i.e. their left hand if they're right handed).

This is difficult! It is a game best enjoyed in the winter months as the smell from some teenage boys' feet in hot weather can be genuinely distressing for anyone in close proximity. And rather than being embarrassed, they are usually more proud than a new mother showing off her baby to a passing elderly person.

Ask students to remove their jackets (and ties if you would like to extend the activity). Working this time in pairs, again only using one hand each, they must replace the items.

Habit makes us really skilful. It is only when we have to try something in a totally new way that we realise how valuable habits are. Habits are useful for straightforward tasks in life but can stifle long-term growth. Working in teams and supporting each other (i.e. being open to new ideas) produces better results on complex tasks.

1⑤ What's the Use?

Time: 5 mins

Additional Resources: none

Students use their creativity and divergent thinking to come up with a myriad of uses for everyday objects

A great opener to get students thinking in a different way, this game never fails to produce surprising results.

In pairs or groups the students must come up with as many creative uses for the object of your choice. You could suggest:

A belt

A box

A paper clip

A bowl

A plaster

When the time is up the students get to feed back their answers. The winner is the group that generates the most creative application. *To give you a flavour We'll take a belt as our object and give it a whirl now.*

A belt could be used as: a piece of rope, necklace, bracelet, dog collar, shoelace for a big boot, lasso, head band, for making a loud noise, weapon, pretend snake, bag strap, sling, bandage, to hold up baggy socks, as a restraint, to slide down a zip wire, to bite on when your leg is being chopped off, missile, stencil for the letter 'O', to measure the amount of spaghetti required ... You get the picture.

The beauty of this activity is you can't get it wrong; you simply have a go. No ideas are to be pooh-poohed, as every idea is valid and must be made note of.

14 'Ave it!

Time: 5 mins

Additional Resources: none

Cockney larfs aplenty in this energy-raising winner

This is a brilliant slant on an old favourite that was passed on to me recently by my cousin Claire Fowler who is a primary school teacher in Leeds.

The class are required to stand or sit in a circle. To pass the energy in a clockwise motion each person (and in their best cockney accent) must shout 'Ave it'. To pass the energy around the other way you must rebuff 'Ave it' by shouting 'Leave it'. To send the energy across the space you must make eye contact and point at someone opposite in the circle and shout 'Oi Roxy', to which that person replies 'Get aht of my pub'. Then the game continues in a clockwise motion with 'Ave it' or until someone decides to shout 'Leave it' or 'Oi Roxy'.

This game promotes energy, openness and focus and is a superb way to start or break up any lesson.

15 Flog the Unfloggable

Time: 10 mins

Additional Resources: none

Students are given the opportunity to think on their feet and use their imaginative powers to influence the group

Split the students into pairs. The task is to come to the front whereupon the teacher will present you with a new product (written on a piece of paper – you won't be required to manufacture a working prototype). They then have sixty seconds to sell this new product to the group. The more ridiculous the product, the more the students will be required to act and think fast.

Give it a go now and try to think of ways you could flog these products:

Cheesy Beer

Leather Socks

Savoury Fruit

Pretend Friend

Rubber House

Edible Car

Encourage the students to think of the products' USP (unique selling point). What are its positives? Could its worst feature be its best? Is there anything like it out there already?

Can they come up with an inventive tagline to promote it? Looking for the positives in any given situation is a tremendous skill and worth developing.

This activity allows students to cut loose and try as hard as they can to make divergent links in a bid to win over an audience – something they will all be required to do many times over when they leave school.

16 Occupational Therapy

Time: 15 mins

Additional Resources: none

Students get to focus in on the person they need to be to do the job they want to do

Ask a student to tell you what job they want to do when they are older.

In groups give the students five minutes to discuss exactly what type of person would be brilliant at that particular job. What skills would they have – are they brave, good at solving problems, motivated, compassionate? What would their personality be like – are they outgoing, kind, mad? Where would they live? How would their friends describe them? How much do they earn? What would the day-to-day job consist of? What would they be wearing? How much training would be involved? What is the best/worst part of the job? What would they do in their spare time? Did they go to university, get a diploma or set up their own business?

Over a very short space of time the class will have built up a profile of the sort of person who might do that job and also what that job might entail. You can then ask the original student if that is the sort of person they aspire to be and, if not, what they would change.

In our experience a lot of young people may say they want to do a particular job because it sounds good or they saw someone on telly doing it. While there is nothing wrong with this, sometimes it pays to really exhaust all the aspects of a profession to work out whether they really like the sound of it or not.

17 The Ultimatum Game

Time: 10 mins

Additional Resources: pretend cash notes (optional)

Students recreate a classic psychological experiment. Will greed or fairness prevail?

Inform students that they are going to recreate a classic experiment. Students should pair up with someone who isn't a close friend. For example, ask people to line up using random factors such as hair colour (darkest to lightest), height, age, alphabetical order (perhaps the third letter of their surname). You could also try this game by pairing friends with each other to see if the results are different.

They are invited to try the following experiment. One person (choose randomly, e.g. tallest, or toss a coin) is asked to imagine they have been given £100 and can offer to share any amount with their partner from £1 to £99. If the partner agrees to take the amount offered, both keep their share. If the partner refuses, neither gets any money. They only get to make one offer. Insist on no talking whilst the student with the money ponders the offer they are about to make. Give out Monopoly money (other board games are available) to add realism. Best not to use real cash, especially if it's yours, as we suspect much of it will go missing. After each pair is finished discuss the results. Who refused? Who accepted? What amounts were offered and why?

In the original study it was discovered that most people offered half or between £40 and £49 to their partner. If the offer was below £20 it was usually rejected meaning neither player received any cash. The experiment contradicts game theory and the standard economics view that people will accept any offer because having something, even a pound, is better than nothing. The experiment shows that people are also interested in fairness and sharing. How do your students compare?

Recent research suggests it may be effective to pay obese people to lose weight. Is this counter-intuitive to our sense of fairness and justice or the same concept as paying unemployed people for not working?

---

18 Alone or Together?

Time: 10 mins

Additional Resources: none

Are humans more successful when they cooperate or when they compete? In this activity students get an answer

Present the following information and question to your students. Ask students to work in pairs or small groups:

Alan makes an axe head in three hours and a handle in four hours.

Beverley makes an axe head in two hours and a handle in one hour.

Are they better off working together or alone? Why?

There are three basic combinations:

1   Working alone Alan would take seven hours and Beverley three hours to make a complete axe.

2   If Alan made two axe heads and Beverley two axe handles and they swapped one each, Alan would work for six hours and Beverley two hours. They would both save an hour compared to working alone.

3   If Alan made two axe handles and Beverley two axe heads and they swapped one each; Alan would work for eight hours and Beverley four hours. They would both work an extra hour each compared to working alone.

Axe head   **Axe handle**   **Axe**

If we assume humans vary in their skills and abilities then cooperation benefits the species. This is a point noted by evolutionary biologists (and hippies). They argue that cooperation has helped humans become such a dominant species. No other species cooperate as much as humans. Axes can be substituted for most objects made by people.

We live in a very social and interdependent world. For example, there is probably no single person in the world that could make a computer mouse. It requires someone to drill for oil, collect it, turn it into plastic, mould it into the shape for the mouse, design the technical parts, attach it, transport it and so on. (Matt Ridley presents the case brilliantly on www.ted.com. If you have fifteen minutes to spare you'll enjoy yourself.)

19 My Round

Time: 5 mins

Additional Resources: one empty 75 cl long-neck beer bottle and a £10 note

The students are set a problem to solve that will test their powers of deduction

This trick is one of our favourites. You simply lay a £10 note flat on a table and place the empty bottle on its head on top of the tenner. You then say to the wide-eyed crowd you have gathered around you, 'This is an incredibly difficult challenge and I bet that no one can whip the tenner out from under the bottle without knocking it over. You can have three attempts: you can touch the tenner but you cannot touch the bottle and whoever is successful can keep the tenner.' This last bit ensures that you never run out of willing participants. It is also a sure-fire way to get everyone in the immediate vicinity pumped full of dopamine (dopamine is a naturally occurring neurochemical that is released in anticipation of or in receipt of a reward). Don't forget though that it is the build-up banter at the beginning of this trick that is the key to its success.

Make a big deal out of this stunt being difficult and play on words like 'whip' and accompany this with a hand gesture; this will suggest that the only way to do this is to use force. Next, you stand back and watch the rusty cogs of invention kick in. It is fascinating to listen to the conversations that will take place regarding angles, speed and force of pulling, not to mention the amount of times you will be asked to repeat the task at hand.

Like any good trick the answer is fairly straightforward but requires the ability to think a little more laterally. As the saying goes 'slow and steady wins the race'. To remove the tenner without knocking the bottle over you simply start at one of the short ends end and roll the note up. Gradually, it will push the bottle off leaving the bottle still standing, your £10 safe, and a lot of teenagers leaving your class thinking you're a smug smart-arse. Trust us, it's worth the effort.

There is a tremendous book we discovered about seven years ago called A Hundred Ways to Win a Tenner *by Paul Zenon and it is crammed full of clever little tricks to confuse, befuddle and more importantly fleece your mates.*

20 A Helicopter Ride

Time: 10 mins

Additional Resources: none

Students are invited to take an imaginary helicopter ride meeting friends around the school to demonstrate one of the most important aspects of wisdom

The teacher reads this script to the students. Students need to settle down first and be quiet.

> I'm going to invite you to use your imagination to demonstrate one of the most important aspects of wisdom. Imagine a small, toy helicopter resting on top of your head. Feel the weight of it and see its colour. Feel your hair move slightly in the draft of the blade as it spins. Imagine a tiny version of you is going to fly the helicopter. Close your eyes and imagine taking control as you fly your helicopter a little above your head. As you hover above your head take a look at yourself through the eyes of you as the helicopter pilot. Fly your helicopter down near ground level and look up to see yourself. What are your thoughts? What do you like about what you see? What don't you like?
>
> Fly your helicopter into the heads of people you like and people who like you. While in their heads, imagine you can read their thoughts. What do they think of you? What do they like most about you? What do they think you could achieve in your life? Fly your helicopter anywhere you want. Find out what you can learn.

This apparently simple activity replicates a method used by creative thinkers (image streaming is described by Win Wenger and Richard Poe in their book The Einstein Factor*), negotiators (Gandhi's version was about walking in his opponents' shoes) and anyone able to* *change their mind about something important such as overcoming a debilitating phobia (in NLP (neurolinguistic programming) it is called dissociation).*

21 Doodler

Time: 5 mins

Additional Resources: pens and paper

Students get to chat without talking and learn to work together in an open and focused way

I first came across this activity whilst working with the education department at Tate Modern in 2008. It is my belief that in order to be truly creative we must first be open; otherwise there is a real risk that we may never produce anything different. Anyone who is looking to form and develop positive relationships knows that the key to this is communication. There are many ways to communicate other than verbally and this activity allows the students to explore openness and to respond and communicate in a more intuitive way.

The class are split into pairs. Each pair has one piece of paper and a felt-tip pen and must decided who is person A and who is person B.

When the time begins, person A must make an intuitive doodle, a line, a pattern or a mark on the paper, then person B must respond to this squiggle with their own doodle. In effect it will become a non-verbal conversation through pictures and shapes.

The key to this working well is not to plan what you are going to draw but to go with it and respond purely to what you see and feel. The results are often very revealing and other members of the class can very quickly work out what sort of conversations/relationships were being formed just by looking at the resulting work.

22 Ten Ten Ten Challenge

Time: 5 mins

Additional Resources: none

Students attempt to solve a puzzle presented to the group to encourage openness

Draw a row of three 10s and ask students: 'Can you make these three 10s answer 950 by adding just one straight line?'

10 10 10

Invite students to have a go. They may need a little bit of encouragement. After two or three volunteers have tried you can reveal the answer.

Answer: Draw a line across the 1 of the middle 10 revealing:

10 To 10

(i.e. 9.50 – the time, 10 minutes to 10, expressed as a number).

Share the learning points of the activity, assuming that nobody guessed correctly. We are often afraid to volunteer for fear of failure, of making a mistake and looking stupid among our peers and the teacher. If we are not open to try things in life we will never learn, grow and develop. Congratulate any volunteers as they demonstrated bravery.

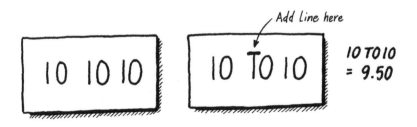

Alternatively, if somebody solved the puzzle, congratulate the person on thinking laterally and being open to thinking differently and creatively to solve a problem. (Thanks to Chris Delaney for this activity.)

Note: It is best to write up the puzzle rather than speak it. If you speak then say 'nine hundred and fifty' rather than 'nine fifty' as the latter version gives a huge clue to the group.

23 Why Are We Learning This, Miss?

Time: 5–10 mins

Additional Resources: none

Students are invited to find an answer to a question probably asked in classrooms across the universe. When we are open and positive we can find useful answers

Has a student ever asked you, 'Why do we need to learn this subject, Miss?' You may ponder the same question yourself on a hot Friday afternoon as your mind drifts to thoughts of your first mouthful of wine that evening. This activity can provide answers for both you and your student.

Ask the student to step forward and draw themselves in the middle of the whiteboard/flipchart sheet. Ask them to identify skills they use in your classroom and add these around their picture.

Some skills may be general – such as communication, listening, working together, researching, summarising – and others subject specific – such as percentages, fractions and algebra.

Ask the student or class to nominate a significant life theme, such as happiness, marriage, global warming, holidays, parenting and so on.

Ask students how the skills listed can assist the chosen life theme. Expect some very interesting as well as some frankly bizarre answers. The result is that your subject becomes more relevant to your students – and you're ten minutes closer to that glass of wine.

Which Would Win?

Time: 5 mins

Additional Resources: none

Students get to justify their decision-making process in an open and focused thought-provoker

We love this activity and have deployed it a lot over the last few years and it never ceases to amaze us how well students can justify even the most bizarre argument. We usually begin with this in a session or employ it straight after a break as a way of getting minds focused back into class.

Ask the students to shout out two random things, for instance, Elephant and Banana.

You then write the objects on the board thus:

Elephant

vs

Banana

Challenge the group to chat in pairs and discuss which would win. Be deliberately vague as the students will have to decide what sort of contest it is. For instance, if it was simply a fight, you may think that the elephant has the advantage, but if it were more about which one is better to nosh on after a long run then the banana may well inch it. As long as the students can justify their response, anything goes.

Remember to explain that they cannot get it wrong – they can only contribute. The great thing about human beings is that there will always be someone to disagree with and so the debate goes on.

This game lets students' thinking loose and more importantly encourages verbal reasoning and asks the question, why do you think like you do?

25 Teacher's Pet

Time: throughout entire lesson

Additional Resources: none

One kid a lesson gets to realise that your talent is in the choices you make

At the beginning you must nominate who will be the teacher's pet for that lesson. From then on whenever you present a question to the group it must go to the teacher's pet first. At this point the teacher's pet has two options:

Have a guess = 1 point

Nominate another student to have a guess = 0 points

Great fun can be had by either having a guess or stitching up their mates. Either way, across a term it means everyone can have a go at choosing to take responsibility for their learning in a bid to gain the most points and officially become teacher's pet.

The overall winner gets an apple/prize of your own choosing from the teacher and a dead arm from their mates.

This exercise enables the students to look at the power of choice and the fact that it doesn't really matter how smart you appear to be, if you consistently make the wrong choices for your life and learning the world will never find out how clever you are.

26 Warm Welcome

Time: 2 mins

Additional Resources: none

Students give each other the time of day

There is no better way to set the overall tone of a lesson than at the beginning.

At the start of the session ask the students to give each other a warm welcome. They will do this by shaking the hand of the person sitting next to them at their desk (or everyone on their table), saying 'good morning' or 'good afternoon' and either giving them a compliment or offering one reason why they are looking forward to working with them this lesson. It is a bit like speed dating for beginners but a lot less awkward and expensive.

This is a little taster that we have used many times and which has helped to lighten the mood and create a relaxed and supportive working environment. What's more, it is simple and effective.

27 Past, Present, Future

Time: 15 mins

Additional Resources: none

Students discuss their successes and in doing so realise how far they have come

We all have days when we think we haven't really achieved much and wonder why we bother. Sometimes it is worth reminding ourselves on a regular basis how much we have achieved and how far we have come.

This activity requires the students to come up with a success or achievement from over five years earlier, one within the previous two weeks and something they hope to achieve in the future.

Once the students have had time to think through their list of three achievements, the activity can then be opened up to the class for debate. Questions such as the following could be asked. What skills did you already have to help you achieve this particular challenge? Did you learn any new skills? Was there a time when you wondered if you would ever be able to achieve it? How did it feel when you did? Other questions such as 'What didn't you do that you could do next time?' can be used to stimulate thoughts and feelings.

This process shows that as unique, complex and sophisticated human beings we are continually developing and refining our skills throughout life, and that only through constant challenge, experience, action and reflection do we truly grow and evolve.

Nose Workout

Time: 10 mins

Additional Resources: two to six small matchbox covers

Students practise energy, openness and focus in this silly game as teams pass a matchbox cover along the line using only their noses in a spirit of cooperation or competition

Divide the group into two or more teams – ideally eight to ten per team. Each team stands in a line with their hands behind their backs. Place a matchbox cover (a small one unless the children have incredibly large noses!) on the noses of the first player in each line. Each player passes the cover down the line, nose to nose. If it falls onto the floor it is returned to the start of the line again. The winning team is the first to pass the cover to the end.

Balloons can be substituted for matchbox covers but this involves more personal areas of the body and is therefore not suitable for all groups.

Balloon Challenge

Time: 5 mins

Additional Resources: a pack of party balloons, preferably mixed colours

Students practise energy, openness and focus in this energetic game in which individuals attempt to burst balloons by sitting on them with force. They don't discover the trick (learning outcome) until the end

Three or four balloons are placed on chairs. Students are invited to sit on a balloon in an attempt to burst it. After the fun and success you can reveal that balloons blown up the most burst easily and those less so are harder to burst. You can make more of this by perhaps having two rounds with different coloured balloons – the first round with balloons easy to burst and the second round with balloons blown up less. Students could be invited to speculate as to why the second round was harder.

Note: Any children conscious of their weight should be allowed to try the balloons that are harder to burst.

30 Potato, Tights and a Balloon

Time: 10 mins

Additional Resources: a potato, a pair of tights and a balloon (per team)

Students practise energy, openness and focus in this daft game to develop the type of purposeless skill in which the British usually excel

The game involves swinging a potato dangling between the legs from a pair of tights tied around the waist. Two teams have to race a balloon across the room without using their hands or feet. Depending on the surface, cheap footballs (smaller size) or small boxes may be more suitable than balloons.

This game could be varied but in essence it is meant to be fun. Just the introduction to this game, 'Today we're going to play a game involving ladies tights, a potato and a balloon' will intrigue even the most battle-weary group of students. Afterwards, the props for this activity can be passed on to your local MP who will be able to use them for a different game.

31 The Roll of the Dice

Time: 5 mins

Additional Resources: a dice

Students learn to summarise their learning following the roll of a dice

This activity is best undertaken at the start or end of a session.

In groups students are asked to summarise a subject, topic or lesson in the number of sentences determined by the roll of the dice. Each group throws the dice separately. The dice definitely adds to the excitement of this activity.

This technique works well following group discussions when tables can summarise their discussion following the roll of the dice.

32 Sitting Up Dead Lions

Time: 5 mins

Additional Resources: none

Students explore relaxed and calm energy in a quiet game which can bond teacher and students

Calm down a group with this challenge. Ask everyone to be perfectly still and quiet. Then offer a prize to anyone who doesn't smile or laugh in the next two minutes. You then try to make everyone laugh by pretending to trip over, looking very closely at a child's face whilst pulling a silly expression, sharing some of your favourite jokes, reminiscing about a school trip or funny thing that happened in class. If you are not a teacher capable of making children smile either change job, enlist the help of a class member or dangle a tights-clad potato between your legs as you chase a balloon across the room.

There are usually a few children in every class who like to have fun and make others laugh. Usually considered disruptive you are giving these children a chance to shine.

This is a version of one of the oldest games played between adults and children – the adult asking the child not to laugh and then making the child laugh. The title is not associated with the latest ill-fated England World Cup campaign.

33 Drinking Problem

Time: 5 mins

Additional Resources: eight matches and a one pence piece

Students have to solve a matchstick puzzle

We have seen this little teaser a few times over the years and we still sometimes forget how it's done.

The matches are arranged in the shape of two glasses (see illustration) and about 10 cm apart. Ask a class member to place the coin inside one of the cups. The other empty cup is only there to add to the confusion – it acts as a distraction because it looks like it must be part of the solution, when in fact it isn't.

The object of the puzzle is to get the coin out of the cup. The catch is you cannot touch the coin – you can only move two of the matches.

Now sit back smugly and enjoy the confusion.

For the solution to this Neo cortex confuddler please see diagram below.

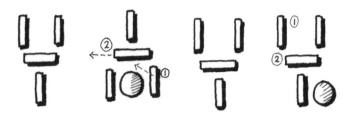

૱૪ What Are You Looking At?

Time: 10 mins

Additional Resources: any objects you see fit or have to hand

Students try eight ways of thinking to discover how familiar things can become invisible

We truly believe that everything is exciting if you look at it for long enough – it is just that a lot of us, either through our educational experiences or upbringing, stop looking. We start to develop apathy and rely on others to do the looking for us or for a teacher to just drop the photocopy into our laps.

So here's what you do. Pick an object such as a shoe. Then on the board write down these headings:

Numbers

Words

People

Feelings

Nature

Actions

Sights

Sounds

The students then brainstorm each of these areas as quickly as possible and write down as many connections as they can muster between 'shoe' and each heading. Before you know it the groups will have created a veritable plethora of ideas, thoughts and connections. You can then invite the groups to feed back their findings to the class.

We have used this system many times with students and teachers and every time without fail we are compelled to look again at everyday objects with a renewed awe and wonder.

This activity uses a technique called 8Way Thinking created by Ian Gilbert, the founder of Independent Thinking, to encourage students to look at things afresh and with a more discerning eye and to prove that everything is fascinating if only you look at it long enough.

35 A Rolf Harris Tribute Band

Time: 5–10 mins

Additional Resources: facility to play clip of Rolf Harris singing 'In the Court of King Caractacus' (available on YouTube)

We dare you to challenge the coolest groups you teach to complete this activity. Energy, openness, focus and memories that will last a long time await

Buy or download a version of Rolf Harris singing 'In the Court of King Caractacus'. The live version is particularly impressive. Have a sing-along and offer a prize to any group or individual who can sing along without making a mistake.

You're unlikely to give out many prizes but you will demonstrate how Rolf himself is cooking on full in the energy, openness and focus department.

36 The Lift

Time: 5 mins

Additional Resources: none

Students explore the role of trust and cooperation within the framework of energy, openness and focus during this quick activity in which pairs of students standing back to back link arms and attempt to sit down and stand up again

Ask the group to line up from tallest to shortest. They pair up with the person they're standing beside (this ensures people of similar height are paired together). Standing back to back they link arms and have to sit down together and then stand up again. Stress that this is not a race – it is a test of teamwork, trust and communication skills.

If students complete the task twice, they'll find it easier the second time.

This activity shows that practice increases our level of performance. If they are asked to complete the task in silence the first time and can communicate during the second attempt then lessons around the importance of communication will be made.

37 Show Business

Time: 15 mins

Additional Resources: pens and paper

Students create a business from scratch

A statistic we came across recently purported that the average student will have between ten and fourteen jobs and within that three to four different careers by the time they are 38 years old. Factor into this that the majority of them will be self-employed in some capacity, then we can be certain of one thing: the world has most definitely changed and more than ever requires our younger generations to be more proactive, versatile and flexible than ever before.

Split students into groups and explain that the challenge is for them to create a business (you may wish to prepare these in advance to save time in the session). For instance, you could give one group an Italian restaurant, one a hairdresser's, one an IT solutions company and one a mobile disco. They then have to flesh out this business by answering questions such as:

What is your business/company name?

What is your mission statement?

How many people work for you?

What sort of people work for you?

How do you develop yourself/your staff?

Is your business local or global?

How many days/hours a week do you work?

What is your salary?

Does your company have a tagline or motto?

When they have done this the groups must feed back to the class. The students then decide which business they would or wouldn't invest in based on the ideas and information given.

This challenge creates an opportunity for the students to think about how to create a business and the questions they may need to ask themselves in order for it to become a reality.

Stare Off

Time: 5 mins

Additional Resources: none

Students get to ogle one another whilst developing their focus

I still love this game and regularly challenge my daughters Rosie and Daisy to a contest. The basic rules are this: on the command 'go' you must stare at your partner without blinking. That's it. You are also not allowed to put each other off.

You may, in a classroom environment, choose to do best of three or get the winner of one pair to join the winner of another pair and keep joining groups until you have the best two left. They can then play the final in front of the class.

As well as being very funny this game also requires a lot of focus and openness to stare at people you may have ignored for three years, not to mention a lifetime's supply of Optrex.

39 Energy Escalator

Time: 10 mins

Additional Resources: none

Students blend energy, openness and focus in this energetic game in which individuals attempt to match a sequence of words with specific movements

A group is challenged to learn a sequence of movements associated with different forms of transport, for example:

Canoe (paddling action)

Plane (arms out like wings)

Car (holding steering wheel and moving it back and forth)

Train (tug bell and say 'choo choo')

Bungee (jump up and down three times)

Once these have been mastered, swap two of the movements around. Alternatively, use the game to demonstrate that we can learn more information if we add movements and fun to the learning process.

40 Clap Together

Time: 5 mins

Additional Resources: none

Students find out how in tune they are with their classmates by clapping

In pairs students attempt to clap in unison with their partner who must speed up and slow down without saying anything.

A more complex challenge is to ask students to clap their own hands together followed by clapping hands with their partner. If they are not in unison it will quickly show.

Students can try this with a close friend and then someone they don't know as well. They are usually far more in tune with their friend. Did this happen in your group? Why?

Encourage students to improve their performance by developing focus (concentration).

41 Plato's Cave

Time: 5 mins

Additional Resources: none

This quick challenge is about what we notice around us and it reveals much about how or what we see or don't see in life generally

Ask students to look around and make a list of everything they see that is plastic in thirty seconds.

Next ask students to close their eyes and write down everything in the room that is metal (i.e. from memory). Their handwriting may not be neat but that's OK. Allow thirty seconds. The first list is usually much longer than the second.

Another version is to ask students to look at all the black objects in the room but then to write down all the green objects.

We always find what we're looking for. This explains why I noticed loads of black Ford Focus cars on the road after I'd bought one but had never noticed one before. In life we do the same. If we look for reasons to be sad or angry or happy we will find plenty. It is not the world around us that determines our mood, it is something generated from within. Plato commented on this thousands of years ago. He suggested that we see life not as it is but as shadows reflected on a cave wall.

Hypno Sits

Time: 5 mins

Additional Resources: none

Everyone gets to sit down (all at once) through intuition and a bit of witchcraft

It is always useful to have several techniques up your sleeve to calm a class and encourage focus. There is no point attempting to teach if half the class are still thinking about break time or what's for lunch.

Ask the entire class to stand up and face the front with their eyes closed. You then explain that only when the whole class is ready can everyone sit down as a group and at the same time. If people sit down at irregular intervals the game starts again. You may wish to try this out a few times with eyes open so everyone gets comfortable with the idea.

What tends to happen is that for the first few attempts some students will be impatient and will try to force the sit or others will get lost in a form of upright daydreaming. But if your group are working well together, and are listening intently and sensing the mood of the room, you will on occasion have a moment where everyone is working together and en masse they sit down at the same time. When this happens you will henceforth be referred to in the staffroom as Gandalf the Great.

It is worth reminding ourselves that learning is not always just about the individual, it's also about the group; and when a group works well, great things can happen. This game forces the class to work as one and relies heavily on intuition and sensing the mood of the group.

Numbers in Letters

Time: 5 mins

Additional Resources: none

Students are challenged to solve two puzzles which develop focus

Ask students to write out the numbers 1 to 10 in alphabetical order.

(Answer: eight, five, four, nine, one, seven, six, ten, three, two).

Ask students what number their name is by making each letter the value of its order in the alphabet (i.e. 1 = a, 2 = b, 3 = c, so David would be 40).

This kind of activity develops our capacity to quickly focus on the more complicated task that follows.

 # Well, I Never

Time: 5 mins

Additional Resources: none

Students share stories

Any relationship gets better the more we feed it and share of ourselves. This activity allows students to share stories, facts and experiences with the class that they will not have heard before.

Announce to the class that they have two minutes to come up with a fact, story or experience that the class does not know about them. The student then feeds this back to the class.

Through sharing these experiences the groups get to discover new things about one another, common interests and more importantly they get to realise that everybody has a life outside of school and that everyone is different. It also proves that no matter how well you know a person, environment, situation or subject, with a little bit of curiosity and the right questions there will always be something new to discover.

Give it a whirl and see what you find out. The answers may surprise you.

45 Book Puzzle

FOCUS

Time: 5 mins

Additional Resources: none

Students respond creatively to a conundrum

Ask your students: 'Why can't you hide a £10 note between pages 47 and 48 of a book with 300 pages?'

The 'real' answer is because books are laid out in a standard format with odd number pages on the right. But students usually have far more creative answers such as:

Because you don't have £10

Because the book doesn't have any numbers.

Because the book only has 46 pages with numbers on and the rest are blank.

Because the numbers have all been crossed out by an evil librarian.

Copy That

Time: 5 mins

Additional Resources: none

Students copy each other's work without being told off

This is an activity that I used to do whilst training to be an actor at the London Academy of Music and Dramatic Art. It was something we were regularly required to practise as a way of building trust and focus.

The hardest element of this task is maintaining eye contact, which many adolescents find incredibly awkward and embarrassing, but it is worth persevering for the best results.

In pairs students can either stand or sit opposite one another. One student is now A and the other is B. Whilst maintaining eye contact student A can begin to move their arms and body (slowly at first). B's job is to mirror as exactly as possible A's movements. When this pattern has been established for long enough the roles can be swapped so B gets to lead.

Seeing as teenagers spend hours in front of the mirror they should be really good at this.

---

47 In the Bin

Time: 2–5 mins

Additional Resources: one bin, one tennis-size soft ball

An energetic activity that gets the whole class on the move

This is one of the most simple yet competitive games to play and combines two techniques in one. First, throwing a ball to select students in a classroom environment is very useful for focus, concentration and hand–eye coordination and also to ensure that the majority of students contribute and that it is not just the same two all the time.

Second, once the student has caught the ball (or it has ricocheted off them and hit three other students in the face, head and privates respectively) you need to get the ball back. That's where the bin comes in.

You explain that on answering a question the student with the ball must now attempt to throw it into the bin. If the ball is successfully rehoused within the bin said student gets to leave before everyone else. If they miss they will remain seated until the bell, like the rest of the class, cosseted in the warm bosom of education.

You may be pleased to know that there is also an accompanying song that goes with this game. It is very easy to learn and in our experience adds to the drama. For your delectation we have included the words below. For best effect sing it to the tune of 'Ere we go! Ere we go! Ere we go!' Start it really slow and get faster and faster as the tension mounts.

In ... the ... bin

In the bin, in the bin, oi, oi

In the bin, in the bin, in the bin, oi, oi

In the bin, in the bin, in the bin, oi, oi

In the bi ... in

In the bin.

Repeat until the ball has been lobbed into the bin.

This game works best with nothing other than 100% conviction and a little dollop of gusto.

 Wing Man

 Time: 5 mins

Additional Resources: none

Students get to sneak a look at each other's work in a game of cooperation and stealth

This activity is a splendid way to review a lesson or to find out how much a group already knows.

You can split up the class into groups or pairs. For the sake of explaining we'll use pairs. Between them they designate who will be the pilot (i.e. in charge and write down all the information) and who will be the wingman (i.e. the scout who will fly missions to other tables to gain intel, ideas and knowledge that can then be debriefed back at HQ, i.e. their table).

I don't know about you but we've just had an overwhelming desire to watch *Top Gun*... We have – and it's not as good as we thought.

This is a lively way to get the students to do all the legwork and encompasses the key invisible elements of this book – energy, openness and focus.

Doodle to Music

Time: 5 mins

Additional Resources: music

Students are invited to daydream to music as a way to stir and release ideas. This is how openness works – when ideas are allowed to flow without being criticised or edited before they can blossom

Ask students to doodle anything that comes into their heads as they listen to a piece of music for two minutes. You could play one minute of stirring music followed by one minute of relaxing music.

🌀 A Golden Ticket for Life

Time: 5 mins

Additional Resources: three sheets of paper (preferably a golden colour and in the shape of a star)

One or more students win an unexpected prize in a game of random luck rather than skill – the format currently favoured by so many TV shows

Before the lesson starts, randomly place one, two or three golden tickets (or yellow A4 sheets divided into squares – sorry to ruin the magic) under chair seats. Prepare yourself for some potentially shocking sights beneath some chairs. If your students always sit at the same seat ask them all to move for this lesson. This in itself is an interesting exercise and an insight into our human nature to avoid change.

Build up a little tension and excitement by asking students to imagine what it would be like to win a lottery. What would be the best prize? Health, wealth, love, fame?

Reveal that there are winners in this class. Some people will be very successful. (Your school may have famous alumni, statistics on how many students become doctors, millionaires or *Big Brother* contestants, etc., so use this information.) Then ask students to look under their seats to see who has won.

Ask the winning students to share their hopes and ambitions with the class. If this ticket meant they could have the life they desired what would they choose? Classmates could be encouraged to offer encouragement and ideas on how the winners could be their best.

Don't we all like the idea of winning something for doing little or nothing?

A raffle win can bring far greater excitement than is justified by the jar of kumquats in fruit liqueur presented to us by the smiling elderly lady who organised the tombola. Why is it we win back a prize less useful and valuable than the contribution we made ourselves? In life the reality is that occasionally, but only very occasionally, we do win prizes for doing nothing. But for the most part effort is rewarded (doh!).

I was recently told a story about a man who approached a well-known shampoo manufacturer and said he could double their sales with just one word. He offered to share it for a million pounds. He was paid on the condition (or conditioner?) it worked. The word was 'repeat' added to the instructions on the back of the shampoo bottle. Although it didn't double sales it did result in enough people washing their hair twice instead of once to ensure he was paid handsomely for his efforts. Not quite something for nothing but not a bad return on an idea that must have flashed into his consciousness in less than a second. I've no way of verifying this story but I hope you'll agree it's a good one, and it does get the cogs turning in your Year 10 groups' heads.

51 Future Intros

Time: 10 mins

Additional Resources: none

Students get to meet their future self

I often wonder what it would be like to meet myself in the future (this is what happens when you don't have any friends). What would I be like? What would I be doing?

Activities for Students

Give the students five minutes to think about and make notes on their future self (let's say twenty years in the future). Ask them to flesh out this person in as much detail as possible.

Then in turn each member of the class must walk to the front and introduce themselves to the group as their future self. The structure below is a good one to follow for the basic introduction.

Good morning/afternoon.
My name is ... and I am ... years old.
I live in (insert country or town here).
I am a (insert profession here).
The best thing about my job is ...
I could never have achieved this without ...
Knowing what I know now I wish I had ...
when I was at school.
Thanks for listening. Bye.

This activity does wonders for confidence and gives the students permission to rehearse their success and feel what it is like to be doing the things they dream of doing. As an add-on you may wish to experiment with a couple of ridiculous intros first to build up class confidence. Why don't you give it a bash now and see where you are in ten or twenty years time?

This game gives the students an opportunity to introduce their future self to the group.

Stand Up, Sit Down, Sit Up, Stand Down

Time: 5 mins

Additional Resources: none

Students get to do exactly what it says on the tin

We love games that are designed to make your brain hurt and this is one of them. It is much like Simon Says and is a quick way to get the class moving, laughing and in a flap. The actions speak for themselves but for the sake of argument we'll explain them anyway:

When you say 'stand up' the class stand up.
When you say sit down the class sit down – they must sit slumped in their chair as if they are in the most boring lesson of all (not yours, of course).

When you say 'sit up' the class have to sit bolt upright wearing the expression of a happy and over-enthusiastic learner (we can all hope).

When you say 'stand down' everyone puts their hands up and shouts 'It wasn't me'.

The fun comes from mixing up the order of instructions or creating a pattern that the students get familiar with only to change it at the last second.

A great way to get the blood pumping and to oxygenate the brain, either at the beginning or midway through a session.

Human Dominoes

Time: 3 mins

Additional Resources: none

A quick puzzle to focus the attention of a group

If five students stand 1 metre away from each other in a straight line, what is the distance between the first and last student?

The most obvious response is 5 metres but the answer is 4 metres. You could demonstrate the answer in the classroom.

54 Chocolate Boxes

FOCUS

Time: 10 mins preparation, then 5 minutes in the classroom

Additional Resources: three boxes (shoe boxes are ideal), three chocolate bars and three labels (slips of paper will be adequate)

Students think inside the box to think outside of the box in this mental puzzle

Three boxes contain one chocolate bar each, a Mars, Crunchie and Wispa. They are labelled 'Mars', 'Crunchie' and 'Mars or Crunchie'. All three labels are wrong. How many boxes do you need to open in order to make all the labels correct?

Answer: none. The box labelled 'Mars or Crunchie' has to contain the Wispa. Therefore the box labelled 'Mars' must contain the Crunchie and the label 'Crunchie' must contain the Mars. Try it out – it works!

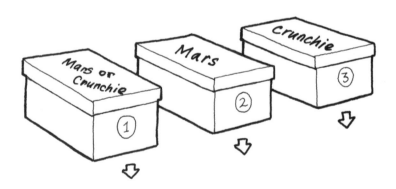

A game that has the potential for students to be rewarded with chocolate tends to be very popular.

55 Alphabetti Never Forgetti

Time: 5 mins

Additional Resources: none

Students get twenty–six keywords from a lesson

Revision is not an option and you can never have enough ways to review a lesson. This is a good one as it requires the students to think of specific words rather than just say the same thing as their mate or other phrases like, 'It was alright', 'I dunno' and 'Can I have my headphones back?'

With five minutes to go, announce that you are going to review the lesson using the letters of the alphabet. As you go around the class each student must then come up with a word that starts with the corresponding letter of the alphabet they are given.

The word can either have been mentioned during the lesson or is in some way feedback regarding the lesson. Random words are not allowed even if they start with the right letter.

This technique promotes quick thought and encourages all the students to contribute in the summing up of a lesson.

56 Building Memory

Time: 10 mins

Additional Resources: none

Recreate a classic method for remembering stuff using your students as VAK (visual, auditory and kinaesthetic) models

Nominate six to nine people to share a different fact or statement with the whole group. This could be six to nine different key points about your subject or random personal information to illustrate the point of this activity (we remember information better if it is made memorable in V, A and K systems). They could stand at the front if this is a large class activity or could work in groups of six to eight spread around the room. Each person shares their fact in sequence. Repeat this three or four times. Part way through the next sequence ask for the group to predict/remember the next fact in line. It is OK for a few wrong answers because, once clarified, these are even more likely to be remembered next time. It helps if facts are delivered in memorable ways such as funny accents or whilst adopting a body posture linked to the fact.

This activity works well with subjects or topics that have sequences of information that need to be learned and remembered. For example, seven students could each deliver a feature of life.

57 Heavy Breathing

Time: 5–10 mins

Additional Resources: none

Students practise the way humans have learned to focus their attention by simply being aware of and controlling their breathing rate

Although we've all learned how to breathe – it is one of the first things we learn and it is something we've done all our lives – like many habits it is an unconscious action. Until we think about it, like now.

Be aware of your breathing now. You're doing amazing chemistry in your lungs exchanging gases; amazing biology feeding millions of cells with energy and life-giving oxygen. It's amazing. If you're 15 you've probably breathed in 240 million times (and breathed out exactly the same number of times – we can put the numbers out of sync by breathing in twice and out once on our next breath). The sequence we learn is in-out, in-out for breathing. There are exceptions. When we cry we generally breathe in a few times for each out breath.

As a quick experiment ask students, whilst breathing at their normal rate, to see how many in-breaths they can take without breathing out. Most people manage around six. This gives us an idea of the amount of lung capacity we use at rest, perhaps one sixth or 16%. This is a nice metaphor for life in general; we use only a fraction of our full potential.

The next part of the activity is basically a relaxation exercise:

Breathe in through your nose slowly and hold for three seconds.

Breathe out through your mouth and
hold for three seconds.

Repeat three times.

On each in-breath ask the group to imagine breathing in fresh clean air and visualise it filling their lungs and body with energy and power to be their best today. On each out-breath they should release tension and negative thoughts from wherever they are in the body, let them drain away, gone. Ask students to focus on the lesson ahead and what they are about to learn.

This effective approach has been used for thousands of years across many cultures and is useful in the classroom.

Semi–Supine and the Schwa

Time: 10 mins

Additional Resources: none

Students get to lie down and make noise in a productive and focused manner

This is another technique that I picked up from drama school which draws directly from the Alexander technique, a method of managing change through the symbiosis of body and mind which was formulated by Frederick Matthias Alexander (1869–1955). For more information check out *The Alexander Technique* by Glynn MacDonald.

Students need to be lying down on their backs with their knees bent up facing the ceiling and in line with their hips.

They must place their hands just under their ribs (which is directly on top of the diaphragm).

Ask them to close their eyes and concentrate on their breathing as this will help them to become relaxed yet alert.

Ask them to breathe in for four counts, and to feel their ribs moving out across the floor, and out for four counts until every last bit of air has gone, all the while making sure they remain as relaxed as possible. Repeat this activity several times.

Some students may find this awkward or are more concerned with what everyone else is up to, but it is worth persevering to get the group into the correct state. Over time and with practice the students will relax into this very quickly.

Once the correct state has been established you can introduce the next phase. This time ask the students to take a deep breath, allow their jaw to relax and drop open and then they are to release one long sustained 'AAAAAAAAAAAAAAAAH' sound. If they are creating the sound from the right place (i.e. their diaphragm) then the noise will be relaxed and open. If they are tense it will sound trapped and will cause tension in the throat.

Phonetically, the clear open sound emitted is called a schwa. All this work enables students to begin developing breath control which is essential in the management of stress and the ability to remain calm and access the thinking brain when the going gets tough.

59 One-Liners

Time: 5 mins

Additional Resources: one piece of paper

Students create a story in two minutes

Start off with a piece of paper with 'Once upon a time ...' written at the top. You pass this to the first student who writes the next line. When they have completed their line they must fold over the top of the paper (covering up 'Once upon a time ...') and only leaving their line exposed. Let this process continue around the class so that each time someone contributes a line they can only see and respond to the line written before and nothing else.

Before you know it you'll have a story and probably a bizarre one at that. You can then choose someone to read it whilst the rest of the group marvel at the wonder of it all.

Openness is the key to creativity and in this activity it is given free rein.

⑥⓪ Here the Drummer Gets Wicked

Time: 5 mins

Additional Resources: none

Students get to make noise and feel what it is like to be in the moment

Many moons ago I used to work for a percussion group called Drum Pulse and this was an activity I had the pleasure of performing with 2,000 delegates at Disneyland Paris. In that instance we had djembe drums, but before you feel any pressure to rush out and stockpile all the hand-held drums in your borough, may I suggest that you either clap or use a desk to create the beat.

For this activity you will need to be the conductor, so start off by establishing a basic beat to the count of four like the one below (beat = clap or tap on the desk):

Beat Beat 3 4

Beat Beat 3 4

Beat Beat 3 4

Once this has been established you can, as the conductor, raise the volume by bringing your right hand upwards or decrease volume by bringing your right hand downwards. If the group are focusing on the beat you shouldn't even need to explain the volume signals, they will just follow you.

When you begin to feel more confident you can then start to play around with different rhythms and patterns like the ones below:

Beat 2 *Beat* 4

Or

Beat Beat Beat 4

Or

Beat 2 Beat Beat

Or if you're feeling really cocky you can double-time it like this:

Beat Beat Beat Beat Beat Beat Beat Beat

You can also add another element here which is to split the room into two so that one side are playing one rhythm whilst the other side are playing a different one. Splitting the room into four means you can practically build an amazing wall of sound that will make other classes wish they were in your lesson.

I have been a drummer for nearly twenty years and recently I met another drummer called Biant Singh who made me look at drumming afresh. He said that when you are drumming you can only ever be in the moment. It is impossible to think of anything else other than what you are drumming. As well as developing coordination, drumming has this amazing ability to focus the mind, bringing everything you are doing into the now, and in this context it galvanises the group to work together and listen effectively to produce a unique sound.

This only goes to confirm what many head teachers have thought for years – if you beat something hard enough you really can produce great results.

61 Moon Walking

Time: 20–30 mins (this activity could be split into two parts over consecutive lessons)

Additional Resources: copy sheets 1 and 2 (below) for each student

Students are asked to rank a series of supplies following an emergency landing of their spacecraft on the moon. First, they work alone and then in a group. Will everyone survive?

Much of the training I received during corporate team-building days were soul-destroying; like living in an episode of *The Office*. However, a few activities were both enjoyable and instructive. The following activities are two of the best.

Invite your students to believe they have been selected to be the first group of students from earth to take part in an exchange visit with a school on Mars. Sadly, on the way to Mars their spacebus has to make an emergency landing on the moon. You are sixty miles from the rescue station on the light side of the moon. All equipment has been destroyed except spacesuits and the ten items listed below.

The game has two parts. First, individually they must rank the items from 1 to 10 in order of importance for survival. Answers to be written in column I. Second, they agree a ranking in their groups or the whole class. Answers to be written in column G.

Supply each student with sheet 1.

The group is then given sheet 2 and asked to transfer their previous ranking scores onto this sheet:

Sheet 1

Rank these items in order, most important 1 to least important 10

	I (Individual's Score)	G (Group Score)
Supply of water for each person		
Oxygen-filled tanks		
Map of moon showing route to destination		
Food concentrate		
Box of matches		
Parachute silk		
Magnetic compass		
First aid kit		
Solar powered heater		
50 feet of nylon rope		

Sheet 2

	Nasa rank	I Score	Diff N I	Nasa rank	G Score	Diff N I
Supply of water	2					
Oxygen tanks	1					
Moon map	3					
Food concentrate	4					
Box matches	10					
Parachute silk	7					
Compass	9					
First aid kit	5					
Solar powered heater	8					
Nylon rope	6					
Total Diff						

Group discussion

First, each person records on sheet 2 the numerical difference between each individual ranking and the NASA ranking. For example: if oxygen is ranked 3 by the individual and 1 by NASA, the difference is 2. Total up all 10 and record at the bottom of the sheet. If your score is low you did well. Also record the difference between your group rankings and NASA's. Was your individual ranking total score lower (and therefore closer to NASA's scientists) than your group ranking score? If so, you were open to be persuaded by group members, so much so that your better answers were disregarded by the group! If your group score was closer to NASA's than your individual score then your openness helped improve your performance. Sometimes in life we are open to other people's ideas and suggestions and sometimes we stick to our own opinions. Neither is always right or always wrong. Knowing when to be open to new ideas and when to stick to our own ideas is one of the most difficult things to learn.

NASA scientists agreed the rankings based on their knowledge of the moon as follows:

1   Oxygen: essential for survival.

2   Water: next most important for survival.

3   Map: required to locate base.

4   Food concentrate: required for energy.

5   First aid kit: important should anyone have an accident.

6   Nylon rope: useful for climbing cliffs and tying injured people together.

7   Parachute silk: useful protection from sun.

8   Solar powered heater: only needed on dark side of moon.

9   Compass: a magnetic compass would work on earth but would be useless on the moon.

10   Matches are worthless as there is no oxygen on the moon to light a match.

---

62   Ready, Steady, Draw

Time: 15–25 mins

Additional Resources: copy sheets 1 and 2 (below) for each pair of students

Students discover the importance of clear instructions in a drawing game

Students work in pairs for this activity. Sitting back to back works well, as does a screen separating both students.

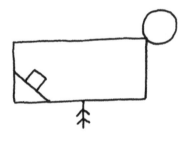

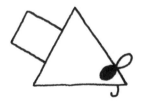

The idea is that one student describes the diagram above for their partner to draw. The partner doing the drawing does not see the template diagram until after they have finished. The describer does not see the drawing as it is being drawn. A three-minute time limit helps ensure the diagram and the drawing have as little in common as Simon Cowell and a good haircut. Swap over for a second attempt using the second illustration and the accuracy increases dramatically.

At the end of the activity students share their experiences.

The learning point is that openness and focus are required to succeed. Good communication requires the feedback missing in this activity.

63 I'm Changing

Time: 5 mins

Additional Resources: none

Students learn without realising that change is uncomfortable

In an ever-changing world, and especially one where technology gets ever faster and life and work is more interchangeable and flexible, it is imperative that our young folk embrace and manage change – to be at the forefront of it so they can leave school and not just cope with life but fully engage in it.

Split the students up into pairs. Each pair must observe the other for about sixty seconds, paying particular attention to how the other looks and what they are wearing. Once they have done this they must both turn back to back and change three things about their appearance. For instance, they may take off a watch, undo a tie or slip off a shoe. It may be worth pointing out that to a particularly boisterous group this instruction may be taken as a green light to a full strip-tease.

Once the three changes have been made the pair can face each other and then hazard a guess as to what changes each other has made. When they have done this they can sit down. When everyone has sat down you can then pose these five questions:

1   Who guessed all three changes?

2   Who guessed two?

3   Who guessed one?

4   Who didn't guess any?

5   Who has put, or is in the process of putting, back what they originally changed?

This last question is fundamental, as 99% of the group will have immediately put everything back as it was. You can then explain that this game is an analogy for change. Sometimes change can be fun, uncomfortable, interesting or a bit weird but at the end of the day we much prefer to slip back into our old ways of doing things. We are creatures of habit and like our routines even if we know they are bad for us or are hindering our progress. All change is unnerving but only through courage, confidence and constant application can we hope to grow and accomplish the things we want to achieve.

This game works as an analogy for change and is very effective.

64 Big Brother

Time: 5 mins

Additional Resources: none

Students have the chance to look at the choices they make and whether they are the right ones

I have been asking the following question a lot recently and the answers have been eye-opening to say the least. The question is this: if you were being watched all the time, what wouldn't you do?

My list was too long to publish but suffice to say I realised that I have several habits that need some immediate attention!

A useful way to deploy this question is to have it already written up on the board as the students come in.

65 Missing Letters

Time: 5 mins

Additional Resources: a random paragraph of text either on screen or paper

Students are given a challenge to measure their ability to switch focus from the specific to the broad and back again

Give students a random paragraph of text and ask them to circle every 's'. Ask them to go back and see if they missed any. They usually do! You can repeat the challenge a few times using the same text. Perhaps ask a question based on comprehension the second time such as, 'What colour was the hat?'

This simple activity demonstrates the narrow way in which we tend to focus our attention at school (focus/convergent thinking). The opposite is divergent thinking/openness. Both are useful.

How Many Triangles?

Time: 5 mins

Additional Resources: copy of illustration (below) on interactive board or on paper

A quick puzzle to focus the attention of a group

Draw out or display the following shape and ask the students to count the number of triangles.

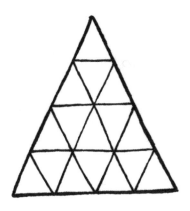

Answer: 35.

67 Tattoo Review

Time: 5 mins

Additional Resources: none

Students learn that body art can be educational

With five minutes before the end of the session, announce that the students must come up with an image or word that best sums up the lesson. They are then to draw said word or image on the back of their hands as a reminder of the key point.

Some of our recent tattoo reviews have included:

Courage

Happy

Future

Fun

Google

Ginger

Who knows, by the end of the week they may look like the bloke from the film *Memento* (if you haven't seen this film then you should. It's excellent!).

This is a really useful way to get students to reflect on their learning because later on they may be doing something completely unrelated and by chance catch a glimpse of the word or may even be questioned about it by a friend or family member.

An Open Exam

Time: 10 mins

Additional Resources: copy exam paper (below) for each student

Students attempt an exam with a difference. Will they spot the 'trick'?

Copy and distribute the following exam sheet to each student. State that they must work under exam conditions and have five minutes to finish. Say that you expect every student to answer all six questions correctly by remaining open.

Exam Sheet

Read all questions before answering.

1   Which of the following is the correct spelling of the condition caused by the recessive gene passed on in the X chromosome?
a. haemophilia
b. haemaphilia
c. haemophillia

2   In 1940 the evacuation of Dunkirk saved how many soldiers?
a. 33,000
b. 165,000
c. 330,000

3   The cube of a number (X^3) is the number multiplied by itself three times (e.g. $3 \times 3 \times 3 = 27$). What is the cube of 4?
a. 16
b. 64
c. 400

4   Haemophilia is passed on through which chromosome?
a. X
b. Y
c. Z

5   In what year did the evacuation of Dunkirk rescue 330,000 soldiers?
a. 1940
b. 1942
c. 1944

6   If the cube of 4 is 64 what is the cube 3?
a. 9
b. 27
c. 81

This is an activity in the value of looking carefully at the detail and reading through all of the instructions before starting – a great exercise to share just before exams. This activity was inspired by the book *The Mysterious Benedict Society* by Trenton Lee Stewart.

In life the answers are all around us. It is just a question of whether we see the answers by looking anew at familiar things.

---

⑥⑨ Peer Inspiration Project

Time: 5 mins followed up in short inputs of up to 5 mins per lesson for one or more lessons

Additional Resources: none

Students derive inspiration from their peers

Few things inspire teenagers more than seeing their peers succeed. Witnessing someone 'just like me' achieve success is a powerful motivator. Look through regional newspapers and collect examples of local children demonstrating qualities such as bravery, loyalty, hard work, altruism and so on.

As a challenge you could ask students to mirror this approach in a simple way by researching local people demonstrating admirable qualities. This could be from their own families or communities. As a step-up you could invite previous students back into school to be interviewed by current students.

This exercise links into Better than the Oscars (Activity 77).

70 Initially Speaking

Time: 5 mins

Additional Resources: paper/sticky notes, pens

Students use their name to revise

With five minutes before the end of the session get the students to use their initials to come up with a useful phrase or set of keywords from the lesson. They can then feed these back to the class.

Get the class to jot their answers down on paper/sticky notes so you can put them on the wall, and with little or no effort you have an instant lesson check.

A quick and useful way to review a session.

7️⃣1️⃣ Spot the Deference

Time: 10 mins

Additional Resources: paper and pens

Students get to explore, focus and reflect on the value of respect

In our dealings with young people the word respect crops up regularly and can often be the catalyst for good or bad behaviour.

Ask the class to write down the word 'respect' in the centre of a piece of paper and then add anything that comes to mind which directly relates to their thoughts and feelings about the word.

You may wish to use the technique 'What Are You Looking At?' (Activity 34) to really flesh out this process.

When they have done this they can feed back their findings. You can further the debate by asking if anyone can give an example of an experience where they have felt respected or disrespected. How did it make them feel? How did they feel about the other person? What didn't they do? What could they do next time?

Next, ask the students to think of someone they respect and list five reasons why. As a group it is interesting to amalgamate the results to find any common threads. Then ask the group what it means to have respect in oneself and feed back these answers.

When all this information has been gathered it may be very useful to put together a list of the things you must do to get respect. This can be put up on the wall for everyone to see and as a constant reminder that to get respect you've got to give it.

This activity hopes to look at what different people mean by the word respect and how in turn this can help with our daily interactions.

72 Story Time

Time: 5–10 mins

Additional Resources: none

In small groups students are given a seven word story (title: one word; story: six words) and are asked to make sense of the story

Split students into small groups and ask:

What's going on?

What do you know after reading the story?

What assumptions can you make when you read the following story?

The story:

Title: Monsters

Story: They knew they needed to move.

The learning point is that 'open' groups generate more ideas – when we are open there are infinitely more possibilities.

For example: 'they' could be monsters considering a move or creatures seeking to move away from (or toward) the monsters; there could be one or more groups of varying sizes (family, tribe, planet); and 'move' could mean move home, place of work, bodies, possessions and so on.

7⑤ The Aliens Have Landed

Time: 10–15 mins

Additional Resources: none

Students have to argue the case for the survival of the human race to an intergalactic group of aliens

The groups are asked to imagine that an alien delegation has landed on earth and each group of students is asked to plead for the human race to join an intergalactic group of worthy species. How would they present their case? What positive qualities do humans possess? Which of these qualities do group members possess? When are humans at their best?

Groups of students discuss the positive qualities humans possess. Energy comes in the form of many different emotions such as anger, love and envy. It is expressed through values such as respect, compassion, hope and imagination.

74 Friends Reunited

Time: every 10 mins

Additional Resources: none

Students get to information–date their mates and focus on learning

Get the students to learn kinaesthetically by requesting that every ten minutes they must move to the next seat in a clockwise motion and then share what they have learnt during the lesson.

In a typical fifty-minute lesson the students will have to review the content five times, which is more than enough to strengthen the synaptic connections in the brain and lay down clear neural pathways for future use.

75 Chewing Gum Stretch

Time: 5 mins

Additional Resources: none (not even chewing gum, before you panic)

Students get to do a physical warm–up using the chewing gum of their choice

Here is a brilliant energiser that was given to me by my best mate Ryan Philpott while he was working with the National Youth Theatre.

Ask the students to stand up. Get them to imagine they are chewing a big piece of gum. Encourage them to really enjoy chewing and moving it around in their mouth. Then suggest they blow bubbles with it – the bigger the better until it bursts. Now propose they bite the chewing gum between their teeth and pull outwards as far as they can, maybe wrapping it around all of their fingers. Then they should take the gum out of their mouth and begin to stretch it in all directions. Ask them to pull it apart as far as it will go and then see if they can get their left leg over the top, then the right leg. Now suggest they roll it up into a ball and throw it to the ground by their feet. They should stand on the gum and then try to lift up their right leg and then their left. Remind them that it is really sticky and strong.

You get the idea – you can play around with this concept all day as long as it enables the students to have a good stretch and a good laugh. See what else you can do with the gum to create more sticky situations.

This is a wonderfully creative way to get students to stretch and physically warm themselves up without realising it.

76 Soap Opera Moments

Time: 5 mins

Additional Resources: none, or prepare cards using the headings/categories below (this will take only 5 mins)

A comedy improvisation game from *Whose Line is it Anyway?*

Groups are given a genre of storytelling and a scenario to act out in the genre presented. The more random and bizarre the combination the better the results.

Sample genres include: romance, comedy, horror, action/thriller, sci-fi, *EastEnders*, Ray Mears, children's TV, wildlife documentary.

Sample scenes include: *Big Brother*, *X Factor* auditions, taking a pet to the vet, a hospital visit, football match, school canteen.

77 Better than the Oscars

Time: 5 mins to introduce, follow-up of 2–5 mins per award

Additional Resources: award certificates/ trophies if required

Students are invited to introduce a rewards system more effective than being paid money

The teacher should consider the logistics within the group before they introduce this activity. Factors such as how often you see the class are important. You could always let your group decide the best way to introduce the idea.

Set up a system for peers to award peers with certificates (for added prestige they could take the form of Oscars or a format suggested by the students). They could be based on values agreed by your class or the whole school such as kindness, respect or humour. Control and ownership should be with the students so teachers need to avoid awarding the certificates. They will mean more when received from their peers. Rules should include that the awards/certificates must be made on the day of the positive act (or as near to it as agreed by the group as realistic) and the giver must present it in class with a short explanation.

This idea is based on a similar system adopted by an engineering company in the US and described in *Drive* by Daniel Pink. The company awarded a $50 bonus, but in these times of austerity we suggest higher values are embraced.

Other researchers report similar results. In a town in the US 50% of residents were asked if they would accept a nuclear reprocessing plant in their neighbourhood by appealing to their sense of civic responsibility. The other 50% were asked the same question but in addition were offered a sum of money equal to 10% of their annual salary to accept the reprocessing plant. Which group were more likely to agree to the plant? What do you think? It was the first group by a significant margin. Money is not the best motivator in many areas of people's lives.

I've had many an interesting discussion on this with groups of teachers and students. When you ask most people what they want in life they say financial security. When I ask why, I'm still to receive a convincing answer. I thought I was sorted recently when a man said he wanted financial security so his children would never have to worry about money. It wasn't until I was driving home that evening and I thought of all the financially secure children of millionaires, such as Paris Hilton, Peaches Geldof and Jack Osbourne, that I realised financial security is not the best thing we can pass on to our children.

Tableau for Four

Time: 5–10 mins

Additional Resources: none

Students get to create still images of the lesson

Towards the end of the lesson explain that the class are going to review the lesson in groups of four. They will do this by creating four different snapshots of the session. Everyone in the group must take part and they have five minutes to come up with the goods and five minutes to present the snapshots back to the group.

As an added extra the students could photograph the tableaux and load them onto the class computer where they could be presented as a slideshow.

A super way to make sure that everyone gets involved in the revision process and not just the confident ones who love an audience.

7⑨ Spellbound

Time: 10 mins

Additional Resources: none

Students get to spell out keywords without saying a word

If you want to get the students to work together and find new ways to communicate other than speaking, this is a great game to start with.

Before the lesson think of some of the keywords that you would most like the students to remember when they leave. Decide on group numbers (depending on the length of your longest keyword). The students then have one minute to spell out the word using only their bodies. Strictly no talking.

This process helps the students to focus, be open and above all develops their muscle memory. If you have a particularly large group which likes a challenge, then get them to spell out the word below as a warm-up:

HONORIFICABILITUDINITATIBUS

According to QI this is apparently the longest word used by Shakespeare (in Love's Labour's Lost) and means 'the quality of deserving honour or respect'.

80 Story Wheel

Time: 15 mins

Additional Resources: none

Students revolve and evolve their creative muscles in this storytelling gem

For this activity you may need to strike all desks to the side of the room. A good bit of cardiovascular never hurt anyone.

The students, each sitting on a chair, need to create an inner circle A and an outer circle B. All of the B's must now begin a story, which can be about anything but to make it slightly more interesting and challenging you explain that their story must involve a carrot (or anything else you decide).

Allow the B's to continue for a couple of minutes then shout 'stop'. The A's must now move around one place so they are opposite someone different. A's must now repeat back to their new partner the story so far but this time, when continuing the story, A's must now add in a submarine (or any other random object/thought) to further the narrative.

This continues for a few minutes and then the A's move around again and this time the B's have to repeat back what they have just heard and then in their retelling must mention something new and bizarre. And so on and so on.

When you feel this activity has come to a natural end it is always worth listening to a couple of the stories to see how different and disturbing they turned out.

This activity works on many levels and encourages the students to think fast, incorporate new ideas and information, listen well, communicate and deal with new people as well as being as imaginative as possible.

⑧① Human Magnets

Time: 5 mins

Additional Resources: none

Students get stuck to everything in a fast paced warm-up

This is another great game to get students physically warmed up and ready for learning. You can have as much fun as you want with this game but you may wish to start off small and build it up.

Get the students on their feet and announce to the group that due to a bizarre accident in the canteen and the release of unidentified gases, their index fingers are now magnetic and are for some unknown reason attracted to their noses. On this remark you must quickly put your finger on your nose so the class follow. Now, try as you might you cannot pull your finger from your nose. The harder you pull the stronger the connection. Your finger then gets attracted to the back of your knee and then to the back of someone else's knee. Then your left elbow suddenly becomes magnetic and is attracted to a desk (whilst your index finger is still stuck hard and fast to the back of someone's leg). Then your whole body becomes magnetised and is compelled to get attached to one corner of the room. This one is brilliant to watch as everyone rushes into the corner of the room and cannot move. You get the idea.

The fun comes from playing around with the notion of attracting one body part to anything else in the room that causes the students to stretch themselves mentally and physically.

 Remote Voice Control

Time: 10 mins

Additional Resources: none

Students get to control each other vocally in an activity to develop focus and communication

Split the class in half and have them standing in two lines facing each other so that everyone has somebody opposite them (about two feet apart).

The first part of the activity looks at communication and how we do it. Let the pairs decide who is A and who is B.

A's start first by saying a chosen line to B (such as a line from Shakespeare's *Romeo and Juliet*: 'Two households both alike in dignity').

Try saying it two feet apart and then gradually increase the distance between the A's and B's by getting the A's to take a step back after each utterance of the line. When both A and B have had a go, discuss with the group what they noticed whilst speaking and watching. What did they do vocally and physically the further they moved away and vice versa?

The next phase is to give the A's control over the B's. Below are signals that A can use to control how B delivers the line:

1   The pitch is controlled by moving the right hand up (pitch is higher) and down (pitch is lower).

2   Volume is controlled by moving the right hand from left to right (far left means quiet, far right means as loud as possible).

3   Speed is controlled by pretending you have a fishing rod. The quicker you reel it in the faster your partner must speak. The slower you reel it in the slower your partner must speak.

Allow the students to have as much fun as they can with this and watch as they develop their vocal dexterity, focus and communication.

May the Force Be With You

Time: 5–10 mins

Additional Resources: none

Optional: show a clip from www.ted.com suitable for older groups

Students are challenged to consider how best to influence people

This activity is inspired by advertiser Rory Sutherland's talks (available to view on www.ted.com). There is a myth that greater force results in greater influence. For example, speed cameras are often in the news and they divide public opinion. Drivers caught speeding face the threat of a fine, penalty points on their licence and even a driving ban. The more recent smiley or sad face signs which flash as motorists pass accident black-spots are only 10% of the cost of speed cameras and carry no penalty. Which do you think has the greater influence on driver behaviour? It is the face; twice as effective as speed cameras at reducing driver speed.

Another example is from Prussia a few hundred years ago. Leader Frederick the Great wanted his people to adopt the potato as part of their diet. He reasoned that with two basic food crops – grain (to create flour for bread) and the potato – his subjects would be less susceptible to famine because if one crop failed the other would come to the rescue. The problem he had was that people hated the potato so much that even passing a law compelling people to grow and eat potatoes proved ineffective. His solution was to decree the potato a royal food only available to the elite. The imperial spuds were guarded by his finest soldiers but he secretly told them to guard the crop badly. Once the peasants thought of the potato in this new way its popularity soared. (The other thing he could have done was to invent chips.)

Challenge your group to think in an open way about other problems and potential solutions. For example, how to encourage the wearing of school uniform or how to get people to change their behaviour and become more green. Sutherland suggests making gas guzzling cars compulsory for convicted criminals thus making them unpopular.

Walkabout

Time: 5 mins

Additional Resources: none

Students explore energy, openness and focus in this punchy and effective warm-up game

Boiled down this is a simple call-and-response activity which requires the students to stay open and take part with gusto.

Clear a space and ask the students to walk about the room in any direction. Whenever you clap your hands they must change direction. Next ask them to make eye contact with someone and not to break it even if they change direction. Then ask them to shake hands and say hello to everyone they meet. Next, give a high five to everyone they meet. Then tell everyone they meet one thing about themselves. Then tell everyone they meet the name of a vegetable, their favourite dinosaur, someone they'd like to be, their favourite dinner, that they love them ...

Once again you can do whatever you like with this activity; as long as everyone is enjoying it and they keep moving you can't fail.

This is a quick and easy game that can be utilised anytime you want to inject a bit of energy into the proceedings.

Should've Gone to Specsavers

Time: 5 mins

Additional Resources: none

Students get to have their eyes tested

When the students are seated and comfortable explain that you have changed five things about the classroom. The students, in pairs, then have three minutes to guess what you've changed.

Despite the fact that the students spend time in this room, when did they last really look at it and take in what is going on around them? We all look but do we really see? To be fully open and focused requires us all to look at things in a different way as if through a new set of eyes. You may be surprised by what you see or miss on a regular basis. To prove this point, go onto YouTube and type in 'awareness test moonwalking bear'.

Chinese Whispers

Time: 5 mins

Additional Resources: none

A student summarises what they've learned in the lesson and passes it down the line. Will it be the same at the end of the line?

This simple version of Chinese whispers allows the main message of a lesson to be repeated by all students in a fun and quick activity. Make sure the person you choose to start the whisper is likely to offer a good answer!

This could also be used at the start of a lesson if you want to recap on the learning from last time.

Jingle Bell

Time: 5 mins

Additional Resources: none

Students create a rhyme to save time

Five minutes before the end of the session ask the students to shout out an even number between one and ten, say four for instance. The students must then construct a four-line jingle that reviews the key message of the lesson before the bell goes. Those that complete a jingle get to say it and then go. Those that don't have one must wait till everyone else has gone. Ha ha!

The students might like to record these jingles on their mobiles as a future learning resource.

A Sweet Focus

Time: 5–10 mins

Additional Resources: a bag of sweets

Students are invited to focus on an object and experience it fully

Hand around one wrapped sweet for each student. Introduce this as a lesson in focus. Ask everyone to place the sweet in front of them and look at it. Encourage them to look carefully and notice more. See the colour, shape and so on. Move on to handling the sweet and noticing its weight, texture and firmness. What emotions are they going through as they visualise eating the sweet? Can they imagine what it will taste like? When they eat the sweet encourage a full experience of the flavours released in different parts of the mouth.

There can be so much to enjoy in simple pleasures. If you're a hippy like me you could even take the group outside to focus on a tree.

Sweet Russian Roulette

Time: 5 mins

Additional Resources: bag of sweets

Students play a version of Russian roulette but with a sweet rather than a bullet

This is a good follow-up to the previous activity. Reveal to students that you are going to give out one sweet to each person but one of the sweets is a trick sweet (the sort you get from a joke shop) and will taste disgusting. The rest of the sweets are normal. Give out the sweets then ask students to look at theirs and describe their feelings to their partner or table. Allow the students to eat their sweet.

I have never used a nasty sweet. Just calling it 'the vomit sweet' tends to grab the attention of a group.

Emotions such as excitement, nervousness, relief and disappointment are usually experienced. Much of life follows a similar pattern.

90 All Tied Up

Time: 5 mins

Additional Resources: at least one school tie

Students get to solve a problem that will tie them up in knots

Set the students the following task. Holding a school tie at both ends, and without letting go, is it possible to get a knot tied in the middle?

The trick is to start with your arms folded (properly) and then grab on to each end of the tie. As you unfold your arms a knot will appear.

This is a terrific way to see how creative the students are at problem solving and whether they have the capacity to think divergently as well as logically.

91 Exit Pass

Time: 5 mins

Additional Resources: none

Students are encouraged to summarise their learning before they are allowed to leave the room

At the start of the lesson announce that students are only allowed to exit at the end of the session if they can share something they have learned or enjoyed during the lesson. This technique encourages students to focus.

This activity works best in the class prior to lunch or home time and is best undertaken at the end of a session.

92 Whose School is it Anyway?

Time: 10–15 mins

Additional Resources: paper and pens

The group explores what they really think about their school (or other grouping)

Is your class/school focused on a common goal or purpose? In this activity you may discover the answer.

Hand each student a sheet of A4 and ask them to write a one-sentence answer to the following question:

What is our school/class purpose?

Students could be invited to share their responses in groups before feeding back to the whole group. Is there consistency within the answers? What purpose would your students prefer? A new school motto could be on the way.

This is an adaptation of a game used in business settings as described by Daniel Pink in his book *Drive*. A variation of the game is to ask students to draw an answer to the question:

If this school were an animal/mode of transport what would it be?

Encourage students to explore their metaphor with questions such as: What is the food/power source? Where do the students and staff fit in?

⑨⑧ Better Ways to Focus?

Time: 5–10 mins

Additional Resources: copy sheet (overleaf) for each student

Students are asked to guess which goal-planning techniques are best

Will they agree with the most recent research findings?

Here are two lists outlining ways to focus on an important goal or ambition:

List 1

■ Make a plan broken into steps

■ Share your goals with people you admire/respect

■ Think about how good you'll feel when you achieve your goal

■ Record and reward yourself for making progress

List 2

■ Think about someone you admire who has achieved the same goal you are attempting

■ Keep your goal to yourself

■ Think about how bad you'll feel if you don't achieve your goal

■ Think about how much other people would admire you if you achieve your goal

Ask students to consider both lists and agree which one, if either, is likely to be more successful. They may use examples of goals their parents or friends have attempted such as weight loss or changing job. They may explore goals they have attained or failed to stick to, such as hobbies and sports.

List 1

1. Make a plan broken into steps

   ....

   ....

   ....

   ....

2. Share your goals with people you admire/ respect

3. Think about how good you'll feel when you achieve your goal

4. Record and reward yourself for making progress

   ....

   ....

   ....

   ....

List 2

1. Think about someone you admire who has achieved the same goal you are attempting

2. Keep your goal to yourself

3. Think about how bad you'll feel if you don't achieve your goal

4. Think about how much other people would admire you if you achieve your goal

Research by Richard Wiseman, described in his book *59 Seconds*, concludes that people who use the methods outlined in List 1 are far more likely to achieve their goals; List 2 activities seem to actually make people more likely to fail.

94 Pull My Finger

Time: 5 mins

Additional Resources: none

Don't panic – it's not what you think!

I have to thank my friend and laughologist Steph Davies for bringing this little nugget of joy into my kit bag.

Ask the students to stand in a circle with their left hand sticking out, palm up to their left side. Their right hand should be held out to the right-hand side in a fist with the index finger pointing down, touching the middle of the left palm of the person next to them. The object of the activity (on the count of 3) is to grab the finger of the person on your left whilst evading the capture of your right index finger by the person on your right.

Sounds complicated, but it isn't. What it is though is hilarious as in general the group breaks out in hysterics as the tension mounts and resolve is broken along with a couple of fingers.

A superb energiser that can be used, at a moment's notice in order to get the students buzzing and focused, all at the same time.

Recipe for Success

Time: 10 mins

Additional Resources: none

Students are invited to share their favourite recipe for a successful future

You may wish to put your own spin on this activity but for convenience we will provide you with an easy-to-use template. The students may want to name the dish after the job title they are after. For example, we will be making an actor, accompanied with educationalist and writer, and a side order of presenter served on a bed of stand-up comedian.

Ingredients

Bravery - 2 very large spoonfuls

Energy - 1 whole packet

Creativity - hundreds and thousands

Openness - ready-rolled

Motivation - pre-prepared

Confidence -
as much as you can find

Method

Blend ingredients together, put into a warm and friendly environment and allow to simmer for ten years. Eventually bring to the boil and serve when ready, making sure there is enough to go round and that everyone gets a taste.

Best served with family, friends and a captive audience.

Warning! May contain nuts.

The students can keep this recipe as a gentle reminder for when things get tough. You may like to create a recipe book filled with all these tasty futures.

My Teacher the Mind Reader

Time: 5 mins

Additional Resources: three (nearly) identical cups or containers

The teacher creates the impression that they can read the minds of their students in a classic scam!

Great magicians harness the power of energy, openness and focus to engage audiences. Many illusions are built around the following basic idea.

Three cups or other containers are placed on a table. You invite a student to hide a personal object beneath one of the containers while you are not looking. Ask them to complicate matters by swapping the positions of the two empty cups. You then look at the cups and predict accurately which cup hides their object.

The effect is made possible by ensuring one of the containers is marked in a subtle way. To guess which cup contains the object you simply look for the marked container. If it is in the same position it must contain the object. If the marked container has moved the hidden object must be in the one position the marked container hasn't appeared in (i.e. the before or after position). Practice this a couple of times and it becomes obvious. This effect can also be achieved with playing cards.

You need to big up your acting skills to maximise the impact. Strain and concentrate as you 'read' the mind of your volunteer. Perhaps claim you are great at reading body language and can tell when someone is lying. (This could be useful later in the year if students think you might be able to read their minds. If you think this is unethical just don't play for money, especially if you work in a primary school. Anyway, you can always reveal your 'secret' at the end of the year.)

97 Focus On Me, Please

Time: 10 mins

Additional Resources: none

Students experience, vote on and practise ways to positively influence others just by the way they speak

The brain has an amazing capacity to conceive and create music, art and inventions when it is focused on a task. True, it also solves problems by accident as well as design, but it is at the moment of focusing that the magic is applied and brought to life. Practising how to encourage others to focus on us and listen to what we have to say is important in life. There are times when we would like to be seen and heard.

This experiment will help students explore three ways to boost their communication skills. Ask students to vote on which approach creates more focus.

Stand still or moving?

Give out an instruction first whilst moving around and handing out paper. Follow up with an instruction whilst standing and making eye contact with some of the students. The vote should reveal the second approach is more effective. An example of this at home would be the difference between a parent shouting from the bottom of the stairs for their child to turn down the music compared to going upstairs and talking face to face and agreeing an acceptable level.

Deep or high pitch voice?

We all have a range within our voice. Let's say our normal voice is 10 on a scale from 1 to 20. Ask the group to count out loud from 10 up to their highest squeakiest voice at 20. Then go back down from 10 to 1, with 1 being their deepest voice, like a voice-over to a horror movie. Give out an instruction with your voice at level 8, then follow it with an instruction at level 12. Take a vote on the most effective. The deeper voice tends to carry far greater authority. The group can practise asking each other to do things with different voices. As an example ask the group if they know when their parents mean business just through the level of their voice and most will say yes.

Aussie rules or not?

A downward inflection at the end of a sentence adds gravity as it is a command whereas an upward inflection lacks gravity as it is a question (except in Australia or the US where there is a tendency to finish every sentence with an upward inflection). Students could practise with the statement, 'I'd really like to borrow your pencil Sheila, as mine is broken.'

These techniques are great for teachers and students as they provide us with the skills to be listened to without resorting to shouting, anger or force.

98 Playing with Perception

Time: 5 mins

Additional Resources: three containers for hottish, warm and cold water. They need to be large enough for a volunteer to immerse their hands

Students experience a trick of perception which messes with reality

Three watertight containers large enough to accommodate a hand submerged in water are each half-filled with water of differing temperatures. One-litre ice cream tubs are ideal. So this game provides the ideal excuse to gorge on ice cream – you're doing it for the kids!

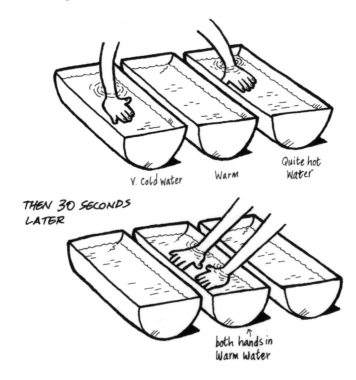

V. Cold water   Warm   Quite hot Water

THEN 30 SECONDS LATER

both hands in Warm Water

In one container place very cold water (add a few ice cubes if possible), in the next lukewarm water and in the third warm to hot water. Volunteers are asked to put one hand in the cold water and the other in the hot water for around thirty seconds (it's longer than you think). They then put both hands in the lukewarm water. They will experience a different feeling of heat in each hand even though the water surrounding both hands is the same.

This is a great metaphor for learning and perception vs reality.

 ## Disappearing Paper

Time: 5 mins

Additional Resources: toilet tissue (A4 paper is an acceptable substitute)

The teacher makes something disappear (and no, it doesn't work with that particular class or student you're thinking about!)

Another trick we can share that is unlikely to have the Magic Circle squirming or calling their lawyers is the disappearing toilet paper. This happens in many school toilets without the use of magic. The teacher should ask the audience not to spoil the trick but just work out if they can see how it is done on their own. The teacher scrunches a piece of toilet paper (or tissue or other light paper). They place it in their clenched hand and ask a volunteer to blow on it three times to make it disappear. Between each blow the teacher theatrically moves their arm around the head of the student and asks them to concentrate hard on making the object vanish and to keep very still. After the third blow the hand is opened and the object has indeed vanished.

The trick is to throw away the object behind the head of the volunteer after the second blow (when the hand is above eye level). Simple but fun. You can add to the impact of this trick by asking for a second student to stand behind the volunteer. Let them know beforehand they are going to catch the object and place it in their pocket or the jacket pocket of the volunteer for a bigger finale.

Things that seem baffling and confusing can be understood once we know how they are done. A different perspective or viewpoint results in different experiences.

100 Money Matters

Time: 10 mins (Part 1), 5–10 mins (Part 2)

Additional Resources: pens and paper

Part 1

Students get a quiz or discussion around the subject of money.

More and more as we work with young people in education we see a huge gap between the kind of life a student wants to have and the job they want to do.

These questions are not set in stone so if you can think of any more feel free to stick 'em in.

1   Average deposit required to buy a house? (we believe it is in the region of £30,000–40,000)

2   How much is the minimum wage? (£5.93)

3   Average income per year? (£25,000)

4   How much would you earn per week working full time in McDonald's? (£237.20 based on a forty-hour week)

5   How much do you get a week signing on? (under-25s get £50.95 or £203.80 a month)

6   Average debt a student will have on leaving university? (£28,000)

7   Average cost of raising a child? (£200,000)

8   Annual income of the job you'd like to do?

This quiz was created to inform students of the financial realities of the world into which they are entering.

Part 2

As a follow-on activity you can explore the link between money and happiness.

We all know that money is the source of unlimited happiness, yes? So here students share their own motivators and recipes for happiness.

If you were to divide out all the money in the world so everyone received an equal share how much do you think each person would receive? According to Michael Neill in his book *Supercoach*, it is estimated that each individual would receive £4 million. Much research suggests that money does not make us happy although many people will disagree when you present this fact. Here are some more money facts:

1% of people in Britain own 25% of the wealth.

Parents spend an average of £700 on presents per child per year.

The average Briton will spend £1.5 million in his or her lifetime.

---

101 Complimentary Gift

Time: 5 mins

Additional Resources: none

Students are encouraged to leave the teacher a parting gift

My daughters attend a school where at the end of the day the students shake hands with the teacher and thank them. I like this simple yet respectful and significant interaction between student and teacher.

This activity takes it one stage further and asks that the students not only shake hands and say 'thank you' but also give one reason why they enjoyed the lesson.

This is both a quick review for the student and a positive confidence booster for the teacher.

102 How Long Will I Live For?

Time: 5 mins

Additional Resources: none

A good question and a game that can be played using statistics and a metaphorical pinch of salt

Students are asked to write down a series of numbers based on their answers to the following questions. They use the numbers to predict their lifespan.

Ask students to make a note of the numbers as you read through the following questions:

Will you get married? (Yes +8, No or not sure 0)

Do you enjoy regular activity? (Yes +2, No 0)

Are you are a couch potato? (Yes -8)

Are you tidy? (Yes +1)

Are you an only child? (Yes -5)

Are you female? (Yes +10)

Are you male and shorter than 1.8m (5' 9')? (Yes +5)

Do you eat mostly fast-food? (Yes -4)

Do you smoke? (Yes -8)

Do you have a pet? (Yes +2)

Do you laugh regularly? (Yes +1)

Are you going to have a good work-life balance? (Yes +3)

Add 70 to the points gained or lost above and you will have an estimate of your likely lifespan.

The above factors can start a good discussion and for most of them we have a real choice which can influence our lifespan. These statistics should be taken with a pinch of salt as we want to enlighten not frighten our students. It is also worth remembering that life is not just about how long we live for; it is also about what we're living for. It's about putting more life in our days not just more days in our life.

For more statistics see The Long Life Equation *by Trisha Macnair.*

103 The Most Valuable Resource

Time: 10 mins

Additional Resources: balloon, hairy head and empty aluminium can

Following an optional demonstration, students are challenged to agree upon or justify the most precious invisible resource

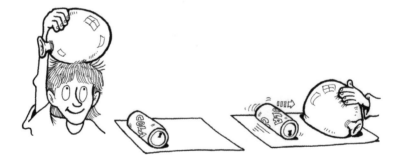

Explain to your group that you are going to demonstrate the power of invisible forces. Blow up a balloon and rub it

against a hairy head (creating static). Place the balloon near to an empty can lying on its side, as illustrated below. Observe the can being pulled toward the balloon.

Challenge students to identify the invisible. There are many invisible forces, things and beliefs: gravity, love, time, hope, consciousness, electricity, oxygen and so on.

John Lloyd, speaking on www.ted.com, eloquently argues that all the most important things in life are things we cannot see. We often ignore or dismiss things we cannot see. This is dangerous as many are the most important things in the world. Energy is all around and inside of every person. Energy can be used to attract or repel people and ideas.

Outro

Outro

Thank you for your energy, openness and focus in reading this action packed tome. Although you find yourself here at the end, it is, metaphorically, just the beginning. Our question to anyone out there who is doing a superb job already, is simply, 'What next?'

We never get to a point where we can simply declaim that we are 'Captain Fantastic and our work here is done'. The world continues to shift and so should we. And so as we doff our cap to the art of 'doing' it is only fair that we challenge you to look ahead and experience a few of the activities from this book for yourself, or with your colleagues, as part of your contribution to an Inset day.

No ifs, no buts, no maybes.

As Indiana Jones said in *The Temple of Doom*: 'Fortune and glory kid, fortune and glory.'

Activities for Teachers

The Flow Test

Learn about flow and when you achieve it in your life

In Activity 5 we offered the flow test as a way to help students identify when and where they achieve flow in their lives. But are you in flow in the classroom? Use the checklist below to find out

Imagine you are in a classroom and around three-quarters of the way through your lesson. You may want to complete the test imagining different classes you teach. If your flow is different ask what is causing the difference.

This checklist is an excellent way to measure flow (a combination of energy, openness and focus) and identify which parts are low and in need of a reset.

Did you have a feeling of 'this is the real me'?

Were you excited?

Were you disappointed when you finished?

Did you think about ways you could do more of the activity or ways you could develop your skill or experience within the activity?

Did you feel energised rather than exhausted?

Did you lose track of real time (time passed more quickly)?

More yes answers relate to higher flow. Flow occurs when our level of skill and the level of challenges we face in a situation are above our average. If the challenges exceed our skill we either grow and develop or crumble and become stressed.

An example of the interplay of these two factors – challenge and skill – was given to me by my son. I asked if he understood the concepts and he compared them to learning a new computer game. At first his skill is below the level of challenges he faces in the game. He is frustrated but keen to continue as he knows his performance will improve with practice. Eventually he is performing really well by applying all the skill and experience he has accrued. He feels brilliant and in control (flow). Later, he starts to become bored with the game because his skill is too high for the challenges the game offers. So can I have another game, Dad?

This explains why researchers find people are in flow more at work than during leisure activities. We tend to choose leisure activities with a level of challenge far below our skill. Exceptions are people who choose dangerous pastimes such as white-water rafting and pot-holing. If you are not convinced you can achieve flow in the classroom read the section in Csikszentmihalyi's book *Flow* on how prisoners of war and prisoners on death row achieve flow.

Future Intros

You get to meet your future self

Give yourself ten minutes to think about and make notes on your future self (let's say five to ten years in the future). Make sure you flesh out this person in as much detail as possible.

Then in front of the mirror introduce yourself to your future self. The structure below is a good one to follow for the basic introduction.

My name is ... and I am ... years old.

I live in (insert country or town here).

The best thing about my job is ...

In order to grow and progress in my current job there are three things I would like to do which are ...

The best thing about my life is ...

I could never have achieved this without ...

Knowing what I know now I am going to make sure that I ... for my own happiness.

Date ....

Tattoo Review

How do you feel right now?

The challenge is to come up with an image or word that best sums up how you feel right now in terms of your life and learning or an action that you will undertake. Now draw the word or image on the back of your hand (or in the space below) as a gentle reminder.

Epilogue

We would love to hear from you after you've tried any of these activities with your students, especially if you can send us a clip to **invisibleteaching@crownhouse.co.uk**

And just a thought before we go. Here are three great reasons to continue doing the job you do:

Number One

Being a teacher is a real challenge –
it is exciting, satisfying and scary. Flow
happens in environments where our skills
are constantly tested and we are in
situations where we have to raise our game;
ten ten ten moments occur more in a
classroom than most other jobs.

Number Two

It is helping to shape the future, developing
human potential and nurturing and
influencing society. Wow!

Number Three

It is a big profession to be part of
and there are loads of opportunities for
personal and professional development in
the UK and abroad.

References

Claxton, Guy (2008). *What's the Point of School? Rediscovering the Heart of Education.* Oxford: Oneworld.

Csikszentmihalyi, Mihaly (2002). *Flow: The Psychology of Happiness.* London: Random House.

Engleman, Marge (2001). *Aerobics of the Mind Cards: 100 Exercises for a Healthy Brain.* Verona, WI: Attainment Company.

Gardner, Howard (1993). *Frames of Mind.* London: Fontana.

Gilbert, Ian (2011) *Why do I Need a Teacher When I've Got Google?* London: Routledge/Farmer.

Gilbert, Ian. '8 Way Thinking' (http://www.independent thinking.co.uk/Cool+Stuff/8Way+Thinking/default.aspx). Accessed 25 May 2011.

Glenn, Jim and Denton, Carey (2003). *Encyclopedia of Family Games.* London: Reader's Digest.

Holden, Robert (2008). *Success Intelligence: Essential Lessons and Practices from the World's Leading Coaching Program on Authentic Success.* New York: Hay House.

MacDonald, Glynn (1994). *The Alexander Technique* (Headway Lifeguides). London: Hodder Arnold.

Macnair, Trisha (2007). *The Long Life Equation: 100 Factors That Can Add or Subtract Years from Your Life.* London: New Holland.

Mosley, Jenny and Sonnet, Helen (2003). *101 Games for Social Skills.* Hyde: LDA.

Neill, Michael (2009). *Supercoach: 10 Secrets to Transform Anyone's Life.* London: Hay House.

Pink, Daniel H. (2009). *Drive: The Surprising Truth about What Motivates Us.* New York: Riverhead Books.

Reeves, Richard (2003). *The Politics of Happiness*. London: New Economics Foundation.

Stewart, Trenton Lee (2007). *The Mysterious Benedict Society*. New York: Little, Brown and Company.

Wenger, Win and Poe, Richard (2000). *The Einstein Factor*. Niles, IL: Nightingale-Conant.

Wilkinson, Richard and Pickett, Kate (2010). *The Spirit Level*. London: Penguin.

Wiseman, Richard (2009). *59 Seconds: Think a Little, Change a Lot*. London: Macmillan.

Zenon, Paul (2003). *100 Ways to Win a Tenner*. London: Carlton Books.

Index

 ## Altered State

 ## Fireworks

Focus

Index

Openness

Praise for *Invisible Teaching*

I love this book – the contents page is like reading the menu at your favourite restaurant – there's so much that is tempting about the chapter headings that it is hard to know where to start first. I tend to choose a pudding before anything else when I eat out and then work my way back through the menu from there – with this book you can do the same. There is no need to read the whole book before you find something you can use and do straight away. Open it at any page and then have a go at an activity or an energiser in your classroom the same day or even half an hour later. Dave and David's enthusiasm leaps off every page and is infectious – I challenge you not to be leaping out of your seat to get on the Energy Escalator or play Sweet Russian Roulette. I will definitely be using lots of ideas from this book to create energy and focus not just with young people of any age, but also adults. There is also lots of scope for using the activities to generate openness and focus at training events and meetings. Invisible Teaching deserves to be a big hit with teachers everywhere.

Clare Smale, Inspired2learn,
trainer, coach and former teacher

As far as education books go, *Invisible Teaching* is fairly unique in that it focuses on a vital but mysterious area of classroom practice: how can you change the atmosphere in a classroom to suit your needs? Outstanding teachers often make these transition phases look easy, but more often than not for most mere mortals it's more luck than judgement. This book provides more than 100 simple but effective techniques to turn this mysterious art into a science.

The book provides a selection of easy to use activities that can be applied to increase energy levels (Year 11 on a Monday morning, anyone?), decrease energy levels (ideal after a lunch on a windy day), improve openness (creativity, lateral thinking, flexibility) or improve focus (looking at things in detail, planning etc.).

All of the activities are designed to be engaging and challenging for pupils, and quick and easy for the teacher to apply. As they aren't subject specific, these techniques can be dropped into pretty much any lesson with any year group.

Easy and enjoyable to read, this book provides teachers with a handy toolkit to dip into whenever the classroom dynamic needs shifting. The authors are clearly passionate about making lessons an enjoyable, interesting place for pupils to learn, and their passion is contagious; I found myself itching to put the ideas into practice. I'm pleased to say that all the techniques I've tried have done exactly what they've supposed to: provided great entertainment, stimulated creative thinking and helped me reshape the learning atmosphere in the classroom.

**Bob Pritchard, Science Teacher,
Woodchurch High School**

A great easy to use book with lots of simple techniques. What I like about books like this is you don't need to read them from cover to cover to get some really valuable quick tips. There's no need for any teacher not to use these techniques and to understand the importance of "invisible teaching". I like the way the book reads, it's clever, but not condescending, it's fun, practical and inspiring.

The ease of use is the most important thing for teachers who need quick fixes in a classroom and I think it does this well. The index is clear and concise and I should imagine when a teacher wants to energise, calm, being more fun into a topic they can plan with this book and use it as a quick remedy to any issues they may be struggling with on any day.

Stephanie Davies, Laughology

This is a book you will want to read cover to cover, it is easy to follow and engaging.The activates I found to be BRILLIANT!, I especially liked how each activity was categorised dependant on your need in the classroom such as the Fireworks, Altered State, Openness and Focus.As a non-teaching member of staff I have been tasked to work with 'Teachers' to engage with the outside world and bring teaching to life and contextualising subjects to how these fit in the world of work. I found each activity 'simple' to implement but 'powerful' in the impact it would have in class. Teachers would find this a useful 'tool' to dip in and out of, especially to engage more with their students and those that embrace and embed some of these activities in their practice will enjoy and welcome the engagement and overall return of their students.

Denis Heaney, Deputy Director of Applied Learning
St. Josephs RC Comprehensive School

This is a cheerful book full of simple ideas to liven up the classroom environment. If you are an aspiring drama teacher, need little ideas for tutor time or are looking for warm ups with a primary age class you will find some ideas that you will certainly want to try out. Many of the ideas will already be familiar to teachers, but there are some new ones that might be appropriate to try out. This book is written in a clear engaging manner and opens with an enthusiastic introduction reminding teachers of the skills we hope to foster in the classroom and why teaching is such a great career.

Caroline Bentley–Davies,
author *How to be an Amazing Teacher*

Invisible Teaching looks at how teachers can control the atmosphere in their classroom and change it to suit their needs. The book offers examples and aims to show that any teacher can control their classroom environment if they use the right techniques.

Included in the book are a range of activities for teachers to use with their students, alongside tips on how to build a rapport with classes and how to promote a positive and focused classroom atmosphere.

The majority of the recommended activities in the book last for five to 10 minutes and can help engage students for the rest of the lesson. They include setting tasks for students to solve puzzles and brainstorms for specific topics.

Both co-authors have a vast amount of experience working alongside teachers in education. Dave Keeling has been a professional actor for 15 years and a "stand up" educationalist for 12 years. Whereas David Hodgson is a training consultant working to motivate teachers and teenagers across the UK, including working with the Institute of Careers Guidance and the Association of Graduate Careers Services.

Headteacher Update Magazine, September 2011

An excellent book which reflects clearly the inspirational and enthusiastic teaching and learning styles of the authors. The activities are adaptable for use at all levels activities 26 and 27 are examples to stimulate group interaction and personal motivation. An excellent book for all schools and colleges to promote engagement and achievement.

John Morris, Director JTM Educational Consultants

This enthusiastic and activity-filled book aims to promote a positive and focused classroom atmosphere by turning regular teachers into brilliant ones via the concept of 'invisible learning'. The authors believe their book can encourage both students and teachers to engage and develop through three main areas of energy, openness and focus. There are more than 100 tried and tested activities to help achieve the secrets of invisible teaching, which require the reader to challenge themselves and be brave enough to try something new.

Leadership Focus, Issue 51 Nov/Dec 2011

Other Books by Dave Keeling and David Hodgson

 Dave Keeling has been a professional actor for 15 years and a 'stand-up' educationalist for 10 years working the length and breadth of the country with teachers, pupils and parents.

 Rocket up your Class!
101 high impact activities to start, end and break up lessons
ISBN 9781845901349

 With Stephanie Davies
The Little Book of Laughter for Teachers
ISBN 9781781350089

 David Hodgson is a Master Practitioner and Trainer of NLP, has the British Psychological Society Level A&B, a Diploma in Careers Guidance and a Diploma in Management. He is a Training Consultant who has worked with companies such as Orange, Walkers Crisps, the NHS, the Institute of Careers Guidance and Association of Graduate Careers Services.

 The Buzz
A practical confidence builder for teenagers
ISBN: 9781904424819

 Magic of Modern Metaphor
Walking with the Stars
ISBN: 9781845903947

 The Little Book of Charisma
ISBN: 9781845902933

 The Little Book of Inspirational Teaching Activities
Bringing NLP into the Classroom
ISBN: 9781845901363

 Personality in the Classroom
Motivating and inspiring every teacher and student
ISBN: 9781845907419